IMAGES
*of Rail*

# RAILROADS OF
# NEW YORK'S
# CAPITAL DISTRICT

**ON THE COVER:** The first 4-8-4 locomotive was made by ALCO Schenectady in 1927, after many steam engine developments had been tested and refined. Since the first batch was made for the Northern Pacific, the locomotive became known as a Northern, although the New York Central called it Niagara. Many consider them to be the most efficient steam locomotives ever produced. Here, a Northern is on the ALCO turntable fresh off the factory floor for an official picture. (Rachel Clothier collection.)

IMAGES
*of Rail*

# RAILROADS OF NEW YORK'S CAPITAL DISTRICT

Timothy Starr

ARCADIA
PUBLISHING

Published by Arcadia Publishing
Charleston, South Carolina

Printed in the United States of America

Library of Congress Control Number: 2020935476

For all general information, please contact Arcadia Publishing:
Telephone 843-853-2070
Fax 843-853-0044
E-mail sales@arcadiapublishing.com
For customer service and orders:
Toll-Free 1-888-313-2665

Visit us on the Internet at www.arcadiapublishing.com

*Dedicated to the late Chris Morley of Ballston Spa, who would
have been proud to see part of his collection featured in this book.*

# CONTENTS

Acknowledgments 6

Introduction 7

1.  Pioneer Railroads 9

2.  Albany and Vicinity 33

3.  Schenectady and Vicinity 67

4.  Troy and Vicinity 89

5.  Changing Times 111

# ACKNOWLEDGMENTS

Many thanks to the late Maurice "Chris" Morley, who let me scan his entire photograph collection before passing away in 2011. The railroad publishing community also lost a valuable member in 2018 with the passing of Jim Shaughnessy, who had a collection of 90,000 photographs, a few of which are included here. Kenneth Bradford provided the photograph archive of his late grandfather, Joseph Smith, which has been crucial in several books. Thanks also to John Nehrich for help with Troy-related captions and access to his research and photograph collection. Paul Garrow's expertise was helpful with Schenectady-related captions. Gino DiCarlo's railroad research came in handy many times. The large collection of photographs (over 35,000) created by the Facebook site Albany, the Way We Were helped point me in the right direction for many of the Albany-related captions. In addition to referencing over 50 history books, I was aided by Tom Tryniski's local newspaper archive of 47 million scanned pages (fultonhistory.com). Rachel Clothier, Corinth historian, let me scan her personal ALCO photograph collection, one of which appears on the cover. Much appreciation is due to the Albany Public Library, Efner History Center (Schenectady), Hart Cluett Museum of Historic Rensselaer County (Troy), New York Public Library, and New York State Archives for their help collecting digital photographs over the last two decades.

# INTRODUCTION

The United States in 1825 was a much different country than it is today. The population of 10 million people lived almost entirely east of the Mississippi River, and the economy was overwhelmingly agricultural, with little heavy industry. Travel between towns was made on horseback, while the export of goods to other states was expensive unless river transportation was nearby.

Clearly the country needed an improved transportation network. The first step was the construction of the Erie Canal across the length of New York State from Albany to Buffalo. When the 40-foot-wide, four-foot-deep canal was opened in October 1825, it was considered one of the greatest engineering projects in history. Since the Mohawk Valley was the only "water level" gap in the Appalachian Mountain range, the Erie Canal provided the cheapest distribution route to the west and quickly became profitable.

As historic as the Erie Canal was, it was soon apparent that trials with land-based steam technology should at least be considered. Speed on the canal averaged four miles per hour downstream and only two upstream. A series of locks that lifted the canal from tidewater to the top of Cohoes Falls was painfully slow to navigate by canal boat even by the standards of the day. The shallow water was frozen for part of the year, closing the canal completely.

The Capital District cities of Albany, Schenectady, and Troy were favorably located to become transportation hubs for early railroads. They stood between the well-settled New England states and the unsettled West, making them a natural pass-through point for hundreds of thousands of people. Vast forests and mineral reserves convenient to the Hudson River allowed for industry to develop in the Capital District and points south. New York Harbor served as an important hub for trade with the outside world and was linked directly to Albany and Troy. The accumulation of wealth in New York City enabled several important projects to be funded, most notably the first canals and railroads.

One of the most overlooked factors in the sudden construction of the first New York State railroads was competition between Albany and Troy, which sometimes bordered on open hostility. Some historians contend that the Mohawk & Hudson Railroad was built to keep Albany from losing more of its trade to the rapidly industrializing city of Troy. Meanwhile, travel to and from Schenectady was painfully slow using the Erie Canal and uncomfortable by stagecoach. Its residents therefore welcomed the concept of a railroad.

While the 1826 charter of the Mohawk & Hudson Railroad was among the first in the country, grading and track laying were delayed for four years. In the meantime, railroads elsewhere forged ahead with the new experiment. Thus, the delays in putting the Mohawk & Hudson into operation for so long meant that it could only claim to be the third common carrier, steam-powered railroad in the country. Nevertheless, it had the distinction of being the first railroad in New York State, the first to be built expressly for steam engines rather than horse power, the first to use locomotives with swiveling leading trucks, and the second to have regular passenger service.

The Mohawk & Hudson proved to be profitable from the start and caused a change in public sentiment, which until then had been highly skeptical of machines that could replace horses. The funding and construction of the Saratoga & Schenectady and the Utica & Schenectady Railroads were carried out in direct consequence to the popularity of the Mohawk & Hudson. These few railroads were quickly followed by many more as investors wanted to cash in on the new technology.

Changes brought by the canals and railroads to cities in the Capital District and points west were dramatic. Between 1850 and 1950, the population of Albany increased from 51,000 to 135,000; Schenectady increased from 9,000 to 92,000; and Buffalo increased from 42,000 to 580,000. In 1840, when there were few railroads in existence, New York had 1,650 miles of tracks in use at an aggregate cost of $65 million, which, along with its series of canals, gave the state the most developed transportation network in the country.

The presence of such a comprehensive rail system by the mid-1800s did much to extend the life of manufacturing in the Capital District beyond what the canals could achieve. For example, the iron foundries of Troy were able to import raw materials direct from the anthracite coalfields of Pennsylvania, the Lake Champlain ore mines, and the ore deposits of the Hudson River Ore Company, near Catskill. Finished iron and steel were shipped to the east on the Troy & Boston Railroad, to the west on the New York Central, and to the south on the Delaware & Hudson and the Hudson River Railroads.

It was unusual for an area the size of the Capital District to have more than one large railroad shop and yard complex. The region's strategic location convenient to New York City, New England, and the West made it an ideal place to host classification yards and repair shop facilities. Comprehensive fabrication and repair shops were built in Green Island, Colonie, Rensselaer, and West Albany, while large freight yards were located in Mechanicville, the Albany waterfront, West Albany, and Selkirk.

Today, there are many railroad buffs in the Capital District who recall the final days of steam in the years following World War II. There were plenty of exciting railroad locations and landmarks at that time, such as the Boston & Albany's main line into the Berkshires; the Boston & Maine's hump yard in Mechanicville; the New York Central's grade and yards at West Albany; the ornate union stations in Albany, Troy, and Schenectady; and the famous Hoosac Tunnel just over the Massachusetts border in North Adams. Rensselaer was a train watcher's paradise with engine terminals, servicing facilities, and yards. The Selkirk yard south of Albany was the site of constant freight activity almost as far as the eye could see. Extensive rail operations continue to the present, including two large passenger stations (in Schenectady and Albany-Rensselaer), the Port of Albany, and the mammoth classification yard at Selkirk.

# One

# PIONEER RAILROADS

Once the Mohawk & Hudson Railroad from Albany to Schenectady proved profitable, other railroad charters quickly followed. A line was built from Schenectady to Saratoga Springs via Ballston Spa in 1832 to take advantage of the large tourist trade stemming from the fame of Saratoga's mineral waters. Troy feared being left behind and in 1835 built a line from Troy to Ballston Spa via Mechanicville. A decade later, the city funded another rail line from Troy to Schenectady.

In 1848, the citizens of Schenectady were among the first to try their hand at locomotive building. After a rough start, the Schenectady Locomotive Works began filling orders in the 1850s and greatly expanded during and after the Civil War.

Albany businessman Erastus Corning, president of the Utica & Schenectady Railroad, organized a convention of railroad owners in 1851. His goal was to unite 10 railroads operating between Albany and Buffalo into one company. After two years of lobbying, the New York Central Railroad was born. It was the largest corporation in America, capitalized at $23 million.

Meanwhile, the Delaware & Hudson Canal Company was diversifying from transporting coal by canals to using railroads. It leased the Rensselaer & Saratoga Railroad in 1871 and commenced building repair shops in Green Island. It also leased the Albany & Susquehanna Railroad from Albany to Binghamton and established a ticket office, freight depots, a roundhouse, and repair shops near the Hudson River in Albany.

The early railroads of the Capital District were among the most important in the country. The New York Central became the famous "Water Level Route" that was able to transport goods and people in the most economical manner to New York City and the west. The Delaware & Hudson, running roughly south to north, became the "Bridge Line" to the Adirondacks and Canada in addition to providing much of New York State with anthracite coal used in manufacturing. The Boston & Albany and the Boston & Maine became the primary outlets for Boston, then one of the country's most important cities, and the rest of New England. By the late 1800s, these systems were firmly established and served as vital transportation systems for the entire nation.

Edward Lamson Henry painted this scene of the Mohawk & Hudson Railroad's first excursion for the Chicago World's Fair in 1893. It depicts the *Dewitt Clinton* locomotive, tender, and three passenger coaches as it began its inaugural trip from Albany to Schenectady in 1831. The event drew crowds from around the region to watch New York's first steam locomotive in action. It was named after the former state governor, who had passed away a few years earlier. The first

trip carrying passengers took place on August 9, while the official opening ceremony, involving politicians and other dignitaries, took place on September 24. Among the guests were railroad president Churchill Cambreling, Gov. Enos Throop, the mayors of Albany and Schenectady, and merchant Erastus Corning, who would one day unite this railroad and others into the New York Central. (Albany Institute of History and Art.)

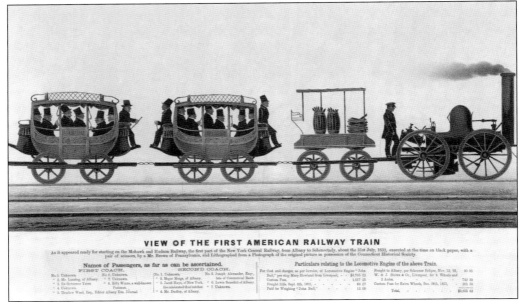

**VIEW OF THE FIRST AMERICAN RAILWAY TRAIN**

As it appeared ready for starting on the Mohawk and Hudson Railway, the first part of the New York Central Railway, from Albany to Schenectady, about the 31st July, 1832, executed at the time on black paper, with a pair of scissors, by a Mr. Brown of Pennsylvania, and Lithographed from a Photograph of the original picture in possession of the Connecticut Historical Society.

This widely circulated silhouette of the *Dewitt Clinton* train is a misnomer. Although it was the first steam-powered passenger train in New York State, several other US railroads began operating earlier than 1831. It also had the wrong excursion date (July 31, 1832) and the wrong locomotive name (*John Bull*), which has since caused confusion in history books. (Library of Congress.)

This c. 1900 photograph of the *Dewitt Clinton* shows an exact replica built at the New York Central's West Albany Shops for the 1893 Chicago World's Fair. It toured the country until the 1950s, sometimes even with actors dressed in period clothing. It is now on display at the Henry Ford Museum in Dearborn, Michigan. (New York State Library.)

When the simple four-wheeled locomotives kept derailing, John Jervis of the Mohawk & Hudson designed a new wheel arrangement, the 4-2-0 (four leading wheels, two driving wheels, and no trailing wheels). He contracted with the West Point Foundry to manufacture one according to his specifications. The *Experiment* locomotive turned out to be so successful that it was soon adopted by other builders. (Author's collection.)

This was the first Schenectady railroad station, built in 1831 by the Mohawk & Hudson at the corner of Crane Street and Third Avenue. This location was known as Engine Hill, as the first locomotives were not strong enough to bring passengers from the city center to the top of the grade. The building later served as a residence but was unfortunately torn down in 1920. (Efner History Center archives.)

The Mohawk & Hudson Railroad's inclined planes were eliminated in 1844 when new tracks were installed starting at the intersection of Broadway and Maiden Lane. The modified route then traveled north along Montgomery Street and west to Schenectady via Tivoli Hollow. All of the original tracks along Gansevoort, Ferry, and State Streets were abandoned. This building served as the ticket office until the first union station was constructed. (Chris Morley collection.)

The *Davy Crockett* was the first locomotive for the Saratoga & Schenectady Railroad, ordered from Robert Stephenson of England and delivered in the summer of 1833. John Jervis of the Mohawk & Hudson designed the "leading truck" concept to keep it on the tracks and recommended it to the Saratoga & Schenectady. The *Davy Crockett* was so successful that an identical locomotive, the *Firefly*, was ordered soon after. (Author's collection.)

The roadbed and rail used by the first Capital District railroads would be considered primitive by today's standards. For the Mohawk & Hudson, heavy stone blocks were embedded in the ground three feet apart and supported by square beds of rubble stone. At each embankment, the rails rested on posts sunk four feet into the ground to minimize upheaval from the changing seasons. (Author's collection.)

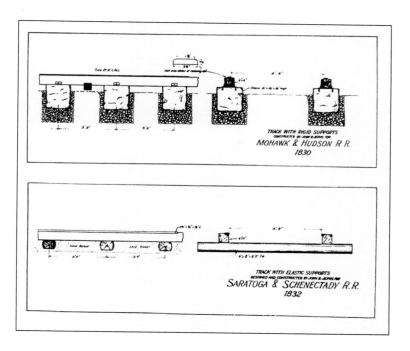

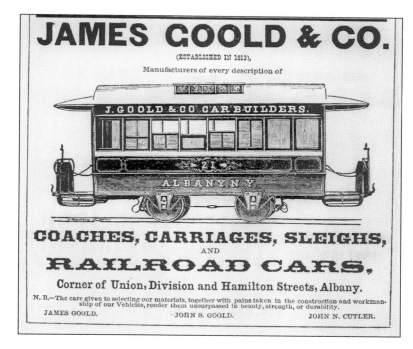

The first passenger cars for the Mohawk & Hudson were merely stagecoaches that had their large wheels replaced with primitive railroad trucks. The coaches were furnished by the carriage and sleigh factory of James Goold, who was well known for his "swell-body" *Albany Cutter* sleigh. Goold delivered six "coach tops" (the contract did not include wheel frames) for $310 each. (1868 Albany City Directory.)

The first passenger station in downtown Schenectady was likely the first "union" station in the country. It was built in 1836 for the Mohawk & Hudson, the Saratoga & Schenectady, and the Utica & Schenectady Railroads near the canal between State and Liberty Streets. It featured Greek architecture that made it seem grandiose for such a small building. The station and adjoining hotel were destroyed by fire in 1843. (Efner History Center archives.)

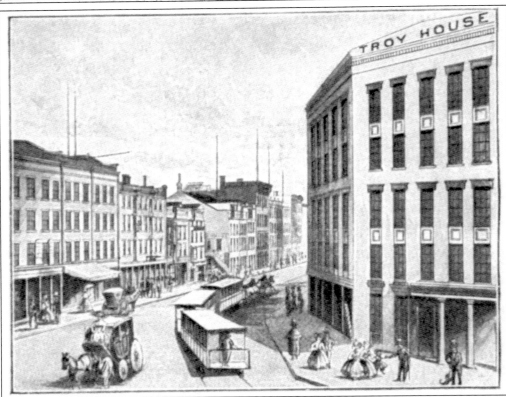

When the Rensselaer & Saratoga Railroad first began operations, the locomotives stopped at the foot of the Green Island Bridge. Passengers were then conveyed across the bridge in railcars pulled by horses to the Troy House on River Street, which acted as the first railroad station in Troy's history. Note the horse-drawn train. (Author's collection.)

# SINGLE MEALS 25 CENTS,

AT THE

# RAIL-ROAD EXCHANGE,

*Entrance Nos. 25 & 27 Maiden Lane,*

## Fronting on Broadway, Albany.

This House adjoins the square used as a Depot by the Mohawk and Hudson Rail Road Company, and opposite the Ticket Office of the Boston Rail Road, and contiguous to the Steamboat Landings.

☞ A Licensed Porter always in attendance.

Board and Lodging, by the Day or Week, on reasonable terms.

ABNER A. POND.

---

An early surviving advertisement related to the Mohawk & Hudson Railroad is this one by Abner Pond, dating to around 1845. His Railroad Exchange served as a hotel and restaurant, according to census records. Living on the premises besides Pond were his wife, four children, and a number of Irish porters, maids, and carriage drivers. (Library of Congress.)

The 4-4-0 wheel configuration was known as the American style and was used by railroads around the country beginning in the 1850s. This Rensselaer & Saratoga locomotive was built by the Schenectady Locomotive Works in 1870 and named the *Commodore Vanderbilt* (No. 37). It was later renumbered by the Delaware & Hudson. (Joseph A. Smith collection.)

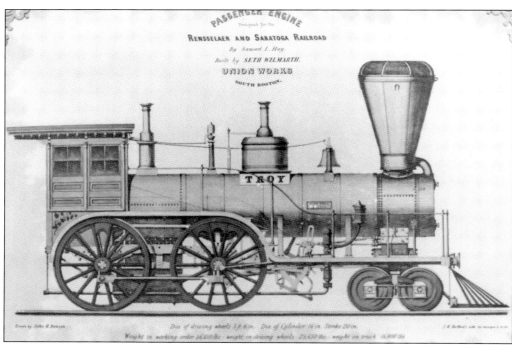

Another example of early locomotives in the American 4-4-0 style is the Rensselaer & Saratoga Railroad's *Troy*, built in 1870 by the Union Works of South Boston. It was more than twice as heavy as the *Dewitt Clinton*, weighing 16,800 pounds. (Joseph A. Smith collection.)

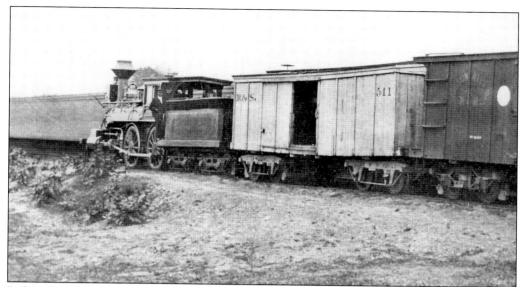

Before the Civil War, trains were short and used wooden, 20-foot boxcars. This Rensselaer & Saratoga train is typical of the 1860s time period. One boxcar is lettered for the Rensselaer & Saratoga, and the other is from the Hudson River Railroad, which served New York City. (Joseph A. Smith collection.)

The wood-burning Troy & Boston Railroad locomotive *Pony* is posed in Troy with its crew. It was used as a switch engine in the small yard and roundhouse on the northern end of the city from 1854 to 1879, when it was traded for another engine. (Joseph A. Smith collection.)

The Troy & Boston Railroad was organized in 1849 to build a railroad from Troy to the Vermont state line through Eagle Bridge. This primitive, hand-powered turntable leads to the two-stall engine house (out of view) near Eighth and North Adams Streets in North Troy. The boxcars are all labeled "T&B RR." (Joseph A. Smith collection.)

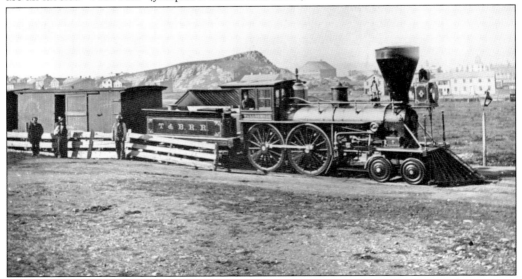

A Troy & Boston train headed by the *Walloomsac* (named after a local river) makes its way through Troy hauling the tiny 20-foot wooden boxcars that were then standard on railroads. The locomotive was built in 1851 and later used by the Fitchburg Railroad. Mount Olympus is in the background. (Joseph A. Smith collection.)

**TROY UNION RAIL ROAD DEPOT.**

*Sixth St from Albany to Fulton St.*

*404 feet long, 240 feet wide x 70 feet high*
*Covering an Area of 2½ Acres.*

The Troy Union Railroad Company was formed in 1851 as a partnership among the major railroads to build a new union station. It was a grand building that occupied a whole city block, fronting Union Street with four suites (one for each railroad company) and office towers on either end. The adjoining 400-foot-long train shed had an arched roof that could hold 10 whole trains. (Author's collection.)

The Rensselaer & Saratoga locomotive *James M. Marvin*, posed here at the Troy Union Station, was built at the Schenectady Locomotive Works in 1867. It was later used by the Delaware & Hudson as No. 125. James Marvin was the proprietor of the United States Hotel in Saratoga and a longtime director of the railroad. (Joseph A. Smith collection.)

The Rensselaer & Saratoga locomotive *I.V. Baker*, built by the Schenectady Locomotive Works in 1867, was named after the president of the New York & Canada Railroad. It continued service after the merger with the Delaware & Hudson, becoming No. 126. (Joseph A. Smith collection.)

# NEW YORK CENTRAL RAIL ROAD.

## WESTERN ROUTE TO
# TROY, SCHENECTADY, UTICA, SYRACUSE,
### ROCHESTER, AUBURN, GENEVA,
### CANANDAIGUA, BERGEN,
BATAVIA, BUFFALO, AND ALL POINTS WEST,

Ticket Office in Albany, Maiden Lane.

GENERAL OFFICE IN ALBANY, EXCHANGE BUILDING.

### OFFICERS:

**ERASTUS CORNING, President.**

| | |
|---|---|
| DEAN RICHMOND, Vice President, | JULIUS A. SPENCER Ass't Sup't. |
| J. V. L. PRUYN, Treas. & Gen. Counsel, | E. FOSTER, Jr., " |
| E. D. WORCESTER, Assistant Tres., | THOMAS WALLACE, " |
| ROBERT L. BANKS, Secretary, | Z. C. PRIEST, " |
| C. VIBBARD, General Superintendent, | WM. G. LAPHAM, " |
| GEO. E. GRAY, Chief Engineer, | H. W. CHITTENDEN, " |
| S. DRULLARD, General Freight Agent. | |

The New York Central was advertised as the "Western Route" and "Water Level Route," since the Mohawk Valley through which it operated was the only gap in the Appalachian Mountain Range. Competing railroads like the Pennsylvania and the Erie had to climb steep grades or tunnel under mountains. (Author's collection.)

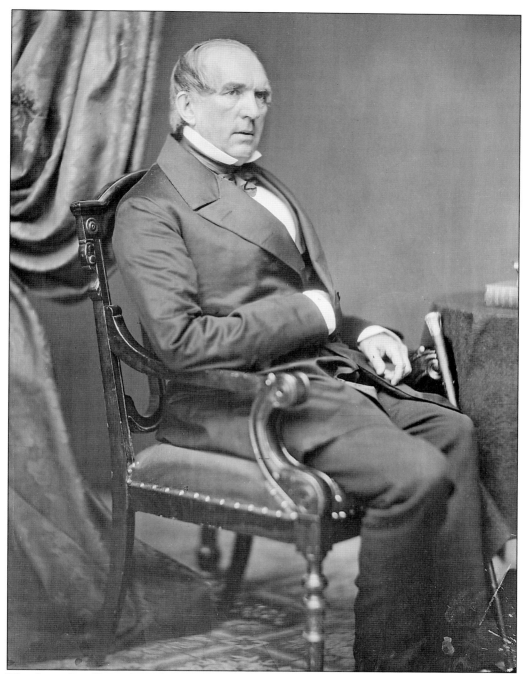

Thanks to the efforts of merchant Erastus Corning, Albany became an important railroad center with some of the most significant rail facilities in the nation. He was heavily involved with local banks, foundries, land speculation, and politics, a combination that made him one of the state's wealthiest men. In 1853, he oversaw the creation of the New York Central Railroad out of 10 minor railroads that spanned from Albany to Buffalo. (Library of Congress.)

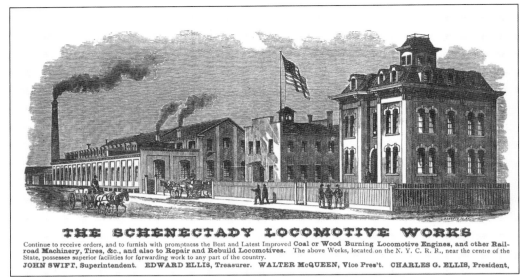

**THE SCHENECTADY LOCOMOTIVE WORKS**

Continue to receive orders, and to furnish with promptness the Best and Latest Improved **Coal** or **Wood** Burning Locomotive Engines, and other **Rail-road Machinery, Tires, &c.**, and also to **Repair and Rebuild Locomotives.** The above Works, located on the N. Y. C. R. R., near the centre of the State, possesses superior facilities for forwarding work to any part of the country. **JOHN SWIFT,** Superintendent. **EDWARD ELLIS,** Treasurer. **WALTER McQUEEN,** Vice Pres't. **CHARLES G. ELLIS,** President.

The Schenectady Locomotive Works got off to a rough start, even with the experience of the Norris brothers of Philadelphia's Norris Locomotive Works. It began operations on present-day North Jay Street in 1848. After the failure of its first locomotive, the Norris brothers departed. At the time of this 1880 drawing, the company had been restructured and was flourishing with 1,000 men employed. (Author's collection.)

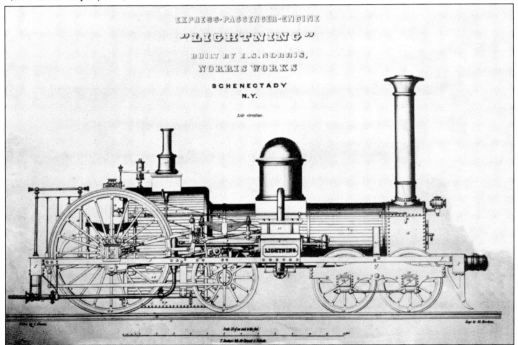

The locomotive *Lightning* was the first ever manufactured by the Schenectady Locomotive Works. It was delivered in 1848 to the Utica & Schenectady Railroad with great fanfare. However, the engine turned out to be too heavy for the lightweight track and had to be retired. This in turn led to a corporate reorganization. (Chris Morley collection.)

24

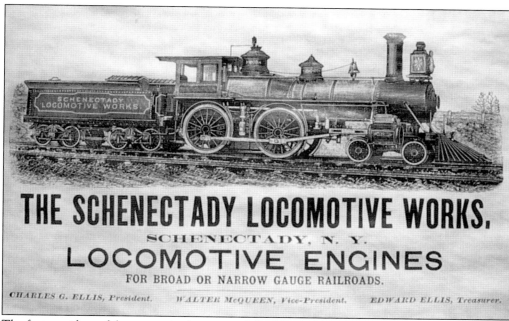

# THE SCHENECTADY LOCOMOTIVE WORKS,

### SCHENECTADY, N. Y.

## LOCOMOTIVE ENGINES

### FOR BROAD OR NARROW GAUGE RAILROADS.

*CHARLES G. ELLIS, President.*　　*WALTER McQUEEN, Vice-President.*　　*EDWARD ELLIS, Treasurer.*

The first president of the reorganized company, John Ellis, boldly began manufacturing locomotives as soon as the Civil War broke out, before there were any orders. The US government soon purchased every last one and requested many more. Various members of the Ellis family occupied the presidency until it merged with the American Locomotive Company. (Author's collection.)

Walter McQueen of the Schenectady Locomotive Works designed an American-style 4-4-0 engine that was simple, practical, and effective. His prototype became so popular that Schenectady locomotives were referred to as McQueen Engines. The one pictured had just rolled out of the shop for its picture in 1868, with others being completed in the background. (Chris Morley collection.)

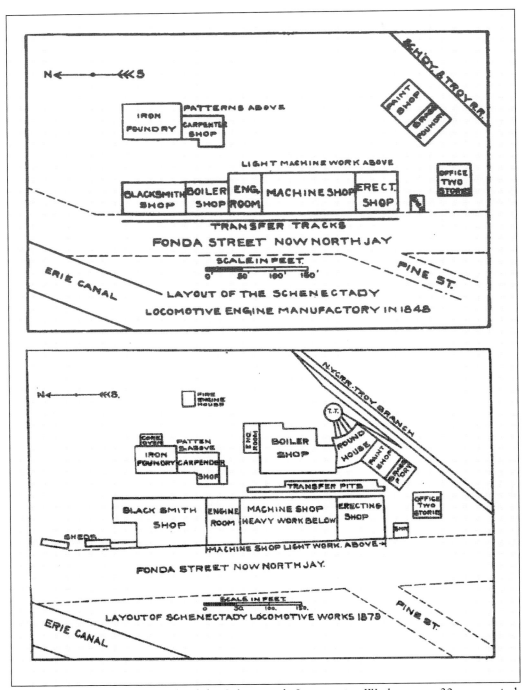

This diagram shows the growth of the Schenectady Locomotive Works over a 30-year period. By the end of Reconstruction after the Civil War, the company had connected directly to the New York Central's main line, added a turntable and roundhouse, and enlarged its other shop buildings. (Author's collection.)

The Schenectady Locomotive Works built four wood-burning locomotives for the Central Pacific Railroad in the fall of 1868. They were named *Jupiter*, *Storm*, *Whirlwind*, and *Leviathan*. On May 10, 1869, the *Jupiter* pulled Central Pacific president Leland Stanford's special train to Promontory Summit in Utah Territory to meet Union Pacific dignitaries for the Golden Spike Ceremony. This famous event marked the "joining of the rails" from the east to the west in America's first transcontinental railroad. (Chris Morley collection.)

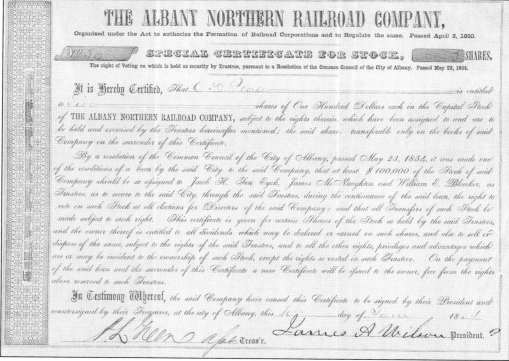

The Albany Northern Railroad was built in 1852 with great promise, running north along the Hudson River through Watervliet, Cohoes, Waterford, and Schaghticoke and ending at Eagle Bridge. However, revenues were not sufficient to cover the high mortgage payment, and the company went into receivership. After a reorganization, the bridge over the Timhannok Creek collapsed in 1859, killing several passengers and causing the company to cease operations. (Joseph A. Smith collection.)

The Delavan House hotel was an Albany mainstay for many years, patronized by visitors disembarking a train next door at the Albany Depot. In 1899, the hotel burned down just as plans were being drawn up for a new railroad station. The valuable riverfront land formerly occupied by the hotel was then used to build the union station that still stands today. (Author's collection.)

The New York Central locomotive *William H. Vanderbilt*, named after Commodore Cornelius Vanderbilt's son and heir, is posed outside Delavan House, which was next door to the Albany Station. It was built by the Schenectady Locomotive Works in 1880, three years after William assumed control of the railroad. (Joseph A. Smith collection.)

This photograph of the Albany Basin in 1869 shows the railroad offices on the left, the union depot in the middle, and a long New York Central freight shed on the right. A track along Montgomery Street ran inside the depot building. The water in front of the depot would later be filled in to create a coach yard. (New York State Archives.)

This is a view of the Boston & Albany yard in Rensselaer, looking west. In the late 1800s, a waterway branched off the Hudson River, circled around the freight yard, and emptied back into the Hudson. The building on the left was known as the Flour House, constructed in 1845 as a freight depot. It was touted as one of the largest railroad buildings in the world at the time, measuring 750 feet in length. (Albany Public Library.)

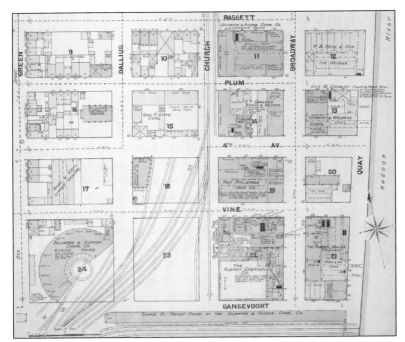

This was the site of the Delaware & Hudson Railroad's first roundhouse (off Gansevoort Street) and repair shops (corner of Church and Bassett Streets). There was also a long freight depot next to the roundhouse that spanned several blocks. Since there was no room for expansion here in the city of Albany, the company built much larger facilities on Green Island. (Sanborn maps, Library of Congress.)

This engraving shows a busy Albany waterfront scene around 1860. The Albany Depot is on the extreme left. In the distance is a sign that reads "Hudson Railroad Ferry; Boston Railroad." At this time, there was no Albany railroad bridge across the Hudson, so passengers disembarking a Hudson River Railroad train on the east side of the river had to be ferried to the west side. (Author's collection.)

On April 25, 1865, the funeral train of President Lincoln arrived at East Albany (Rensselaer), just 11 days after his assassination. The coffin and its escort were ferried across the river while the train proceeded north in order to cross the river at Troy and come back south to Albany. After a daylong service and procession, the coffin was brought to the waiting train car at Broadway (pictured) and departed by train to Buffalo. (New York State Archives.)

Due to resistance from the City of Troy, ferryboat owners, and other interests, a railroad bridge across the Hudson River at Albany was not constructed until 1866. At first it was called the Hudson River Bridge or Lumber Street Bridge. In 1902, it was rebuilt and the name for Lumber Street had changed, so thereafter it was called the Livingston Avenue Bridge. (Library of Congress.)

There are so few pictures of the pre-1900 version of the Albany Depot that a lithograph must be used to get an idea of what it looked like. The building was shared by the New York Central, the Boston & Albany, and the Delaware & Hudson Railroads. Next door was the Delavan House and various freight sheds along the Albany Basin. (Library of Congress.)

The Fitchburg Railroad consolidated many rail lines in New York, Vermont, and Massachusetts. Locomotive No. 139, seen here at the North Troy freight yard, was built at the Schenectady Locomotive Works in 1879 for the Troy & Boston; it later became Boston & Maine No. 1097. It was scrapped in 1908 after an impressive 30 years of service. (Joseph A. Smith collection.)

# Two

# ALBANY AND VICINITY

Of the four major population centers that made up the Capital District in the 1800s—Albany, Schenectady, Troy, and Saratoga Springs—Albany seemed to reap the most benefits from the arrival of railroads. It became known as the "Western Gateway" through which nearly all people and goods heading to the western part of the country passed.

Erastus Corning, who masterminded the creation of the New York Central in 1853, established a large locomotive repair facility along with a car classification yard at West Albany. Next door he built the 100-acre Albany Stockyards to store and slaughter animals for distribution to the east. In 1880, the stockyards handled almost 48,000 carloads of cattle, sheep, and pigs.

Cornelius Vanderbilt of the Hudson River Railroad made national headlines when he blocked the new railroad bridge from Albany to Rensselaer in the winter of 1866. This was done when directors of the New York Central reneged on the terms of a contract. Vanderbilt ended up assuming control of the Central after accumulating shares when the stock price plunged. Over the next decade, he invested heavily in upgrading track, stations, and freight facilities as well as acquiring railroads to the west, making the New York Central one of the nation's most important railroads.

The Delaware & Hudson established its corporate headquarters in Albany with the 1912 construction of extensive locomotive shops in Colonie and the 1915 building of a new office complex near the banks of the Hudson River. The Albany waterfront was also home to the Albany Union Station and a New York Central freight terminal. Just across the river in Rensselaer were the roundhouse and locomotive facilities for the Boston & Albany as well as New York Central roundhouses and yard.

Albany was famous for its wide variety of businesses, which were primarily served by the New York Central and the Delaware & Hudson. In 1900, there were 2,200 factories in Albany County employing 25,000 people. Albany's breweries, lumber district, stove foundries, and the Watervliet Arsenal were well known and contributed greatly to the volume of trains, numbering in the hundreds, that stopped in the city each day.

As president of the New York Central, Erastus Corning obviously had tremendous influence as to where the railroad's repair shops would be located. Over the objections of other large cities such as Syracuse and Rochester, Corning designated his home city of Albany as the primary railroad hub. The locomotive and car repair shops eventually employed thousands of people and was the largest rail facility in the Capital District until the Selkirk Yard was built. (New York State Archives.)

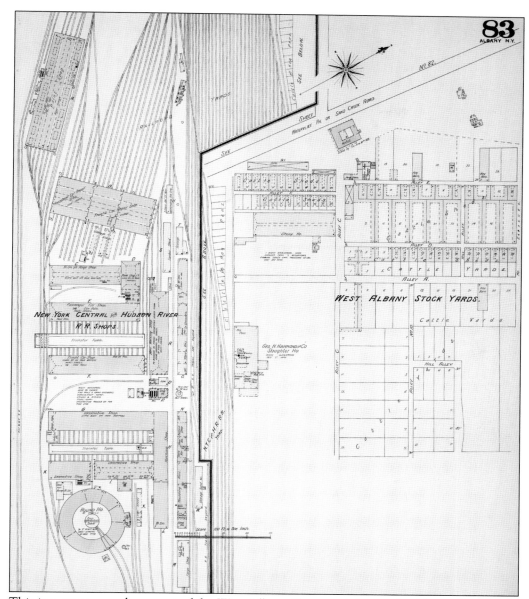

This insurance map shows part of the West Albany Shops and the nearby Albany Stockyards. The New York Central allocated 700 cars for hauling cattle from western states to be slaughtered and processed in Albany before being shipped to Boston and other eastern cities. Nearby was a hotel for workmen and a slaughterhouse. The locomotive and car repair shops used transfer tables to move equipment to one of the 80 stalls. (Sanborn maps, Library of Congress.)

For about 100 years, the facilities at West Albany provided steady work to as many as 6,000 people at any given time. Posing for this c. 1950 photograph are employees of the coach shop, which repaired, maintained, and rebuilt passenger cars. (Chris Morley collection.)

The array of shops and factories at West Albany required a team of managers and administrators. This 1937 photograph is titled "Supervisors, West Albany Car Shops." Rows of spare car wheels are lined up against a shop building in the background. The shops and yard initially occupied 250 acres of land, purchased in 1854, and were later expanded to 350 acres. (Chris Morley collection.)

# They keep a
# SuperServiceStation
## for New York Central Locomotives

THE run ends. Engineer and fireman climb down from the cab, and a "hostler" takes over. Under his expert hand, 350 tons of pulsing steel move obediently off to the roundhouse . . . that super-service station for locomotives.

Here, mechanics, electricians, pipefitters, specialists in many crafts work day and night . . . inspecting, repairing, lubricating and adjusting the streamlined "Hudsons" and mighty "Mohawks" of

New York Central's motive power fleet.

Today, with modern machines and electrical aids, they're cutting precious hours from maintenance time . . . keeping engines longer on the job to move the vast war traffic. And tomorrow these roundhouse teams will apply their war-born efficiency to servicing the still finer locomotives now taking shape in the designing rooms and testing laboratories of New York Central.

**PARTS DEPARTMENT**
Roundhouse "Storekeeper" normally has thousands of engine parts on hand. They range from huge driving wheels to tiny springs for the Valve-Speed Indicator . . . a modern device that keeps a safety and efficiency record for each locomotive.

**LOOKING "UNDER THE HOOD"**
Locomotive front swings open and Inspector steps into the smokebox for examination of the interior. Rigid check-up keeps New York Central engines working efficiently despite heavy war loads.

**A GOOD TURN IN WARTIME!**
Girls operate many roundhouse turntables. With more than 26,000 New York Central employees in armed services, more women are needed for railroad jobs.

**"CHECK THAT WIRING!"**
On a modern New York Central steam locomotive, Electricians have many things to check . . . from the headlight to the electric Train Stop, the wonderful guardian that would halt train *automatically* if danger signal were passed.

**LUBRICATION JOB— LOCOMOTIVE SIZE!**
Roundhouse Grease Cup Fillers use lubricating guns so large they are moved about on wheels. Grease and oil are forced out by high pressure air from nearby power house.

**ELECTRIC "DETECTIVE"**
Before invisible cracks in steel can grow and cause a breakdown, Machinists locate them with an electric detector called the Magnaflux. "An ounce of prevention is worth tons of cure," on New York Central.

**"CHANGE THOSE TIRES!"**
Locomotives have steel tires. When tires need changing, electric Drop Table lowers 52 tons of driving wheels and whisks them to service track . . . 50% faster than old methods of wheel removal.

**FREE! NEW, ENLARGED BOOKLET,**
"Behind the Scenes of a Railroad at War"—13 cutaway pictures of 20th Century Limited, caboose, engine cab, troop train, mail car, hospital train, etc. Write Room 1223H, 466 Lexington Ave., New York 17, N. Y.

# NEW YORK CENTRAL
## THE WATER LEVEL ROUTE

**BUY MORE WAR BONDS**

NEW YORK CENTRAL SYSTEM

This advertisement for the West Albany Shops during World War II shows a breakaway of one of the large roundhouses that were used to service steam locomotives. At this time, more than 26,000 New York Central employees were fighting in the war, prompting the company to advertise for female workers. (Chris Morley collection.)

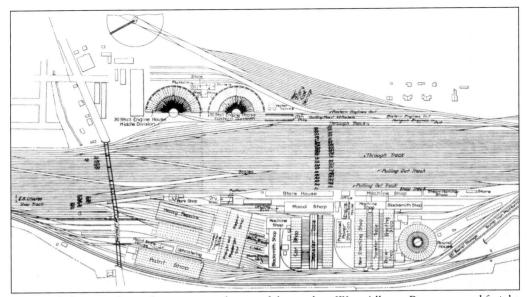

This track diagram shows the impressive layout of the yards at West Albany. Passenger and freight tracks paralleled one another as they approached the yard from the east (right). A curve to the left carried the passenger tracks to the south of the shops, while a sharp curve to the right carried the freight tracks to the north and ran through the facility in an unbroken tangent. The sorting yard was broken up into a series of "pockets" that were worked by a single engine and crew that were unhampered by movements in other parts of the yard. (Author's collection.)

Former president Ulysses S. Grant passed away at Mount McGregor in Wilton (Saratoga County) on July 23, 1885, just days after completing his memoirs. Workers at the Delaware & Hudson Green Island Shops draped black crepe over a new 4-4-0 passenger locomotive numbered 210, which was chosen to convey the funeral train from Saratoga to Albany. A New York Central locomotive then took the train to New York City. (Joseph A. Smith collection.)

Albany was one of the greatest lumber markets in the country from the mid- to late 1800s. Most of the lumber came from Canada, the Great Lakes, and other parts of New York State. A horse railway was used to service the district at first, but later the Delaware & Hudson added a switch and spur track that ran along the east side, next to the Hudson River. The main line ran along the west side toward Menands. (Chris Morley collection.)

The Maiden Lane Bridge was constructed in 1870, a few years after the Livingston Avenue Bridge. Sometimes known as the South Bridge, it was constructed to allow passenger trains access to the Albany Union Station on Broadway. At the other end of the bridge in Rensselaer were rail facilities for the Boston & Albany and the New York Central Railroads. (Albany Public Library.)

The Albany Basin is in need of some revitalization in this 1890 scene. The photographer is probably standing on the recreation pier. Two Delaware & Hudson boxcars and a few flatcars are being loaded along the riverfront, at the foot of State Street. On the left is the store of paper stock dealer Henry Stoll, located at 16 Hudson Avenue. (Albany Public Library.)

As the capital of New York State, Albany has hosted many legislators coming and going throughout its history. Once the railroads were established, the New York Central and the Delaware & Hudson began running special "legislative trains" with upgraded passenger cars. Adam's Temperance House is next door to the Delavan House, while the dome of Stanwix Hall is at far left, on the other side of the depot. (Author's collection.)

George Daniels of the New York Central was a tireless promoter of the company. He conceived of the idea for an express train from New York City to Buffalo with limited stops and ordered the West Albany Shops to build a locomotive specifically designed to pull a passenger train at the highest possible speed. The result was engine No. 999, the most famous locomotive in the Central's history. In 1893, it reportedly attained a speed of 112.5 miles an hour, faster than any vehicle in history up to that time. Below, it is seen pulling a replica of the *Dewitt Clinton* in Albany on one of its many publicity tours. (Both, Chris Morley collection.)

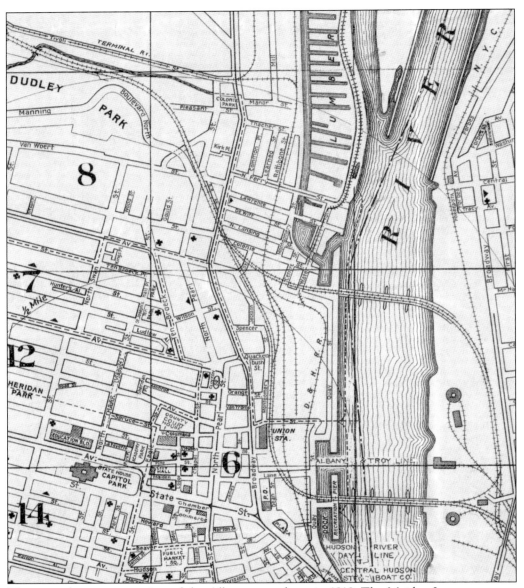

This map shows an overview of the Albany waterfront in 1919. The Maiden Lane passenger bridge is on the bottom, while the Livingston Avenue freight bridge, which bypasses Albany Union Station, is above. On the right (east) side of the river is Rensselaer, with simplified track plans of the Boston & Albany yard and roundhouse (top) and the New York Central yard and roundhouse. To the north are the Delaware & Hudson Railroad tracks leading to the lumber district and its boat slips. The solid lines through State Street and Broadway are trolley tracks. (Library of Congress.)

The volume of passenger trains arriving and departing Albany every day required a new, larger union station. In 1899, the Boston-based firm Shepley, Rutan, and Coolidge was selected by the New York Central to design a suitable building to be shared by four railroads. The Beaux-Arts-style granite structure featured arched openings that led to a waiting room with 110-foot-high ceilings. (Library of Congress.)

A close-up view of the Albany Union Station around 1920 shows the covered entrance on Broadway. Automobiles, horses, and a United Traction trolley car are all in use. This picture reflects the height of railroad operations in Albany as the country experienced a post–World War I prosperity but before the Castleton Cut-Off project, which rerouted trains south of the city. (Albany Public Library.)

As one entered the Albany Union Station waiting room, a men's barbershop, bathroom, and smoking room were on the left with the baggage room just beyond. To the right were the women's lounge, the restaurant, and its kitchen. Opposite the entrance were the parcel room, ticket office, newsstand, and telegraph office. The general waiting room was meant to convey the importance and wealth of the railroads at this time. (Albany Public Library.)

As a junction point for several railroads, the Bull Run Yard adjacent to the Albany Union Station was the site of constant activity. Locomotives would be changed out on through trains, strings of cars were disassembled and reassembled, and westbound trains were given pusher engines for the steep climb up West Albany Hill. (Albany Public Library.)

This aerial photograph of the Albany waterfront yard shows a rare view of the other side of the Hudson River in Rensselaer. On the right side of the Maiden Lane Bridge is the giant New York Central roundhouse, built in 1927. Behind it is the engine terminal and coaling tower. On the left side are the well-known Flour House freight depot and the Boston & Albany yards. (Fairchild Aerial Surveys, New York State Archives.)

The Hudson Navigation Company and other steamboat lines built concrete docks at Albany's Steamboat Square in 1915. The *Berkshire*, pictured docked at the port, was built in 1908. The McEwan coal pocket is right of center. The Albany-Greenbush Bridge, precursor to the Dunn Memorial, is in the background. (Library of Congress.)

Here is a 1930s overview of the New York Central's Albany riverfront passenger yard (on the right) and the extensive Bull Run freight yard. The large building on the bottom left is the Morton coal pocket, the largest coal storage facility in Albany. It was remodeled from a New York Central grain elevator in 1900 to hold 20,000 tons of coal. (Chris Morley collection.)

Water Street lived up to its name in this flood scene. The tracks of the Delaware & Hudson ran close to the Hudson River, resulting in periodic floods until the Sacandaga Reservoir was built upstream in the 1920s. The small, 10-post building labeled "Murray's Line," left of center, was a barge company that operated at the foot of Hudson Avenue. It exchanged freight with the Delaware & Hudson Railroad. (Chris Morley collection.)

46

Here is an overview of the New York Central's rail yards in front of Albany Union Station (center). The Bull Run Yard was used for freight and could hold 500 cars, while the passenger (coach) yard closer to the station could hold a little over 200 cars. Citizens complained that the railroads blocked their access to the river, much like they do today about Highway 787. (Albany Public Library.)

Delaware & Hudson "camelback" switcher No. 30, built by ALCO in 1903, is moving some boxcars past the Weidman, Ward, and Company wholesale grocery warehouse around 1920. The building on the right is the Blue Ribbon Potato Chips factory, one of the first of its kind in the country. This location is on Broadway at Westerlo Street, near the present-day Dunn Memorial Bridge. (John Nehrich; Delaware & Hudson collection.)

This view is from present-day Erie Boulevard looking west over the Delaware & Hudson tracks toward Broadway. Tivoli Street is on the right. Both of these buildings still stand, and the faded lettering of Albany Terminal Warehouse can be seen today. The warehouse was built near the famous Van Rensselaer family estate. (Albany Public Library.)

In 1892, Benjamin Babbitt established a factory in South Albany producing lye, caustic soda, household cleaners, and plumbing specialties. By the early 1900s, almost 200 men and women were employed at the three-building complex. Much of the output focused on Bab-O kitchen cleanser, used by housewives around the country. The factory buildings, located on the banks of the Hudson River near Broadway and Fourth Avenue, were served by the Delaware & Hudson. (Albany Public Library.)

The Beverwyck Brewing Company was one of the most successful of its kind in Albany's long brewing history. It was established in 1878 and was one of only three that survived Prohibition, finally closing in 1972. The New York Central main line and bridge over Broadway are at the top of the photograph. Note the boxcar at the Erie Boulevard side of the complex, off the Delaware & Hudson main line. (New York State Archives.)

The shipment of coal from Pennsylvania to New York was the Delaware & Hudson's primary reason for existing. The McEwan Coal Company built this structure in 1906, and it was capable of holding 3,600 tons of coal brought in by the Delaware & Hudson. Screens were used to separate the various sizes to be sold for the appropriate application. Even the coal dust was sent downriver to the brick factories. (New York State Archives.)

Francis C. Huyck established a mill in Rensselaerville for producing paper makers' felts, blankets, and wool jackets. After a fire in 1894, he moved the business to the city of Rensselaer off the main line of the New York Central. The sign on the building reads, "Huyck Kenwood Wool Products." Across the Hudson River in the background is the faint skyline of Albany. (New York State Archives.)

During the early 1900s, the Huyck Kenwood Mills expanded into one of the largest felt manufacturers in the country. The New York Central main line and small yard is on the right, while the Hudson River can be seen at upper left. The present-day Third Avenue Extension passing over the railroad is in the foreground. This area is now the site of the Albany-Rensselaer train station. (New York State Archives.)

Since the downtown area near the Albany Basin was so congested, businesses began to be established north of Albany along the railroad tracks. This became known as the Warehouse District. A long spur track off the Delaware & Hudson main line ran along the entire length of Tivoli Street to serve the warehouses there. (Albany Public Library.)

The Albany Packing Company was established on the north side of the West Albany freight yard in 1924. It was later known as the Tobin Packing Company, famous for its Tobin's First Prize name brand. Tobin's location on Exchange Street gave it easy access to the New York Central, one reason it remained competitive well into the 20th century. The 32-acre site shut down in 1981 and has since been vacant. (Chris Morley collection.)

The Albany Car Wheel Company was established in 1902 on Thacher Street to produce chilled car wheels for steam and electric cars. After relocating to Broadway, it expanded to manufacture almost 25,000 tons of car wheels annually. Unlike many other iron and steel foundries in the region, it was able to survive the Great Depression and beyond, finally closing down in the 1960s. (Albany Public Library.)

Inventor James McElroy formed the Consolidated Car-Heating Company to manufacture his patented railroad car heaters, door closers, switch panels, and lighting systems. George Westinghouse, inventor of the railroad airbrake, was an early investor. The name was later changed to CMP Industries and survives to this day in its 1890s-era production building on North Pearl Street. (Albany Public Library.)

In 1882, the Hudson River Aniline and Color Works was formed in Rensselaer. Its product line of dyes was expanded to include medicine when it was acquired by Bayer Corporation in 1903. Rail sidings can be seen snaking into the property from the main line. The road running diagonally is the Columbia Turnpike, while the Port of Albany can be seen across the Hudson River. (New York State Archives.)

The warehouse and retail store of Montgomery Ward in Menands was opened in the spring of 1929. Within a decade, there were 1,200 employees at the site, which was one of nine warehouses situated around the country. In 1930, the Delaware & Hudson handled 1,600 cars inbound and 2,100 cars outbound at this location. (New York State Archives.)

The hamlet of Dunsbach Ferry in Colonie was an important Mohawk River ferry crossing and had a small waiting station built by the Troy & Schenectady Railroad. The station was located at the Dunsbach Ferry Road intersection, just south of the present-day Interstate 87 Twin Bridges. Today, this track bed is part of the Mohawk Hudson Bikeway. (Kevin Franklin, Town of Colonie historian collection.)

Long before the current Albany-Rensselaer Station, there was a New York Central passenger station in Rensselaer, located near the Maiden Lane Bridge. The tracks encircling the station are the New York Central and the Boston & Albany main lines to freight yards and engine terminals. (Joseph A. Smith collection.)

The hamlet of Altamont received its first combination passenger and freight depot in 1863 by the Albany & Susquehanna. The Delaware & Hudson built the pictured station in 1897, and it served until passenger operations were discontinued in the mid-1960s. Happily, the building still survives as the Altamont Library. (Author's collection.)

Here is a quintessential steam railroad scene in 1920s Altamont, complete with station, water tower, crossing tower, signals, yard, passenger cars, boxcars, and coal shed. The Altamont Hotel is on the right. (Chris Morley collection.)

Delmar was formerly known as Adamsville, named after early settler and hotel owner Nathaniel Adams. In order to convince the Albany & Susquehanna Railroad to build a passenger station in such a rural place, his son John contributed half the funds needed in 1866. The separate freight station was built in 1908. The house in the distance still stands. (Susan Leath, Bethlehem town historian collection.)

Railroad workmen are seen repairing the tracks at Adamsville, facing east toward Albany. The arrival of the railroads had a significant impact on local citizens. For example, in 1866 one could purchase a 20¢ ticket and hop on the train in Adamsville and arrive in Albany 15 minutes later. This was a far cry from hitching up the horses and braving the rough, winding roads for an hour's ride. (Chris Morley collection.)

The elegant Slingerlands station, with waiting shelters on either side, was built by the Delaware & Hudson in 1888. The freight house, built in 1864, formerly served as both a freight depot and waiting station. When the new passenger station was built, the little depot was moved across the tracks and remodeled. (Author's collection.)

The small hamlet of Elsmere was named after a popular novel titled *Robert Elsmere*. The Albany & Susquehanna's tracks came through in 1863, but there were not enough people to justify a passenger station until the 1890s. This photograph is looking east with a view of the small station and freight siding. (Chris Morley collection.)

West Troy (Watervliet) became a manufacturing center beginning in the early 1800s. The Albany Northern built the first station in 1852 on the west side of Genesee Street. It was remodeled as a residence when a new station was built in 1874, which itself was replaced by the pictured combination station near the intersection of Twenty-Third Street and Tenth Avenue. (Hart Cluett Museum of Historic Rensselaer County collection.)

The Watervliet Arsenal, on the Delaware & Hudson main line, has manufactured armaments for the US military since 1813. At first the Hudson River was used to transport finished weapons, followed by the Erie Canal. When the railroads came, spur tracks were constructed off the main line and into various buildings so the heavy shipments could be loaded with cranes. Shown is Building 110, known as the "Big Gun Shop." (Library of Congress.)

The small passenger and freight depot in Meadowdale was built in 1864 by the Albany & Susquehanna Railroad. It was officially known as Guilderland Station but was referred to as Meadowdale by the Delaware & Hudson in its advertising to hikers visiting Thacher Park. This was the only stop between Voorheesville and Knowersville until passenger operations were discontinued in 1931. (Author's collection.)

The hamlet of Fullers in Guilderland had only about 60 residents, but through the efforts of town supervisor Aaron Fuller, the West Shore Railroad built quite a substantial station in 1883. Its presence caused Fullers to grow dramatically, and soon there was a blacksmith, general store, grammar school, hay business, feed store, and post office. Up to eight trains stopped here daily to pick up high school students or deliver mail. (Albany Public Library.)

The first Voorheesville railroad station was built in 1864 by the Albany & Susquehanna. In 1890, the New York Central, the West Shore, and the Delaware & Hudson built this union station, featuring a distinctive roof that resembled a witch's hat. A freight depot was located on the other side of the tracks that received thousands of tons of hay and straw from area farmers. (Chris Morley collection.)

Here in the northeastern part of the country, snow often played a major factor in railroad operations. Until wedge plows and rotary snow blowers were developed, tracks had to be dug out by hand. This typical winter scene is in Voorheesville, facing toward the small freight station. (Chris Morley collection.)

Three miles north of Voorheesville, the US Army purchased farmland and built an extensive Army depot to receive, store, maintain, and distribute military equipment. It was first used during World War I, expanded to its greatest extent during World War II, and discontinued in the 1960s. (Albany Public Library.)

In 1866, the Saratoga & Hudson River Railroad connected Ravena with Schenectady. Later, the West Shore constructed a rail line from New Jersey to Albany via Ravena. A station (pictured), roundhouse, and homes were built soon after as the community grew. The freight yard declined after the Selkirk Yard was built, but the station survives as the Department of Public Works. (Joseph Boehlke, Ravena-Coeymans Historical Society collection.)

The centerpiece of a project to redevelop the Albany waterfront in 1915 was a large office building primarily occupied by the Delaware & Hudson. Albany architect Marcus T. Reynolds was hired to design a grand structure that eventually consisted of a 12-story tower flanked by wings and extensions. The costly ornamentation of the exterior, serving no practical purpose, is a testament to the vast wealth generated by the railroads. (New York State Archives.)

A view of the Delaware & Hudson office building looking east shows the Maiden Lane Bridge and Albany Yacht Club. As of this 1925 photograph, the Albany Basin has not yet been filled. A United Traction trolley car is making its circuit around the plaza looking for passengers. (Fairchild Aerial Surveys, New York State Archives.)

In conjunction with building the Delaware & Hudson administrative offices was the construction of a new and enlarged freight house on one wing along Dean Street. This 1930 winter view over Broadway shows the freight house on the right. The elevated tracks on the left are coming off the Maiden Lane Bridge. (New York State Archives.)

This aerial view of Ludlum Steel (left) also shows a large part of the Delaware & Hudson Colonie Shops (top right). As larger locomotives and freight cars came into service, it became apparent that the three Delaware & Hudson shops at Green Island, Oneonta, and Carbondale, Pennsylvania, would no longer be adequate. Therefore, a mammoth new car shop and engine terminal was constructed just west of Watervliet in 1912. (New York State Archives.)

Locomotive No. 536 is being overhauled inside the Delaware & Hudson Colonie Shops in 1937. The largest building was the 200,000-square-foot locomotive shop, which was designed to service the longest locomotives in existence. Rather than slow-moving transfer tables that moved locomotives from one bay to another, giant overhead cranes were used. Other cranes were located outdoors to move materials between buildings or other outdoor locations. About 2,500 workers were employed here at the height of operations in the 1920s. (Chris Morley collection.)

Delaware & Hudson president Leonor F. Loree was known for his experiments with a wide variety of steam locomotives. Shown is a "Mother Hubbard" (also known as camelback) style engine, No. 53, in Albany, manufactured by ALCO Schenectady. ALCO made 27 of these for the Delaware & Hudson between 1902 and 1903. (Joseph A. Smith collection.)

The Delaware & Hudson Consolidation locomotive No. 1219 was originally built by ALCO Schenectady in 1918. Twenty years later, it was rebuilt at the Colonie Shops as the first all-welded boiler on a locomotive in the United States. (Joseph A. Smith collection.)

The hamlet of Groesbeckville was on the southern outskirts of Albany. It was described by one publication in 1859 as a "squalid suburb of Albany" but was later incorporated into the city itself as the population grew. The hamlet was mostly residential housing, but some industries were served by the Delaware & Hudson Railroad, such as these buildings on South Pearl Street near Second Avenue. (Albany Public Library.)

A track gang is installing new rails along the Delaware & Hudson main line north of Albany in 1937. Track maintenance was an unglamorous but essential part of operating a railroad. Just north of here was the two-story Menands Station, built in 1877. (Chris Morley collection.)

# *Three*

# SCHENECTADY AND VICINITY

Schenectady's location in the Mohawk River Valley made it destined to be a transportation hub of great importance. The first railroad in the state was built from Albany to Schenectady in 1831, and others soon followed. The growing city became the termination point for the Saratoga & Schenectady (1832), the Utica & Schenectady (1836), the Troy & Schenectady (1847), the Saratoga & Hudson River (1866), and the Schenectady & Susquehanna (1872).

The manufacturing sector of Schenectady was greatly enhanced by the Erie Canal and multitude of railroads. Thomas Edison established General Electric in Schenectady due mainly to the city's first-class transportation lines, while the Schenectady Locomotive Works was created to serve the rail industry directly and became the second-largest employer in the city. After merging with other companies in 1901 to form the American Locomotive Company, the Schenectady branch remained an important manufacturing site until the late 1960s, sometimes employing 6,000 people. Schenectady became known as "The City that Lights and Hauls the World," derived from these two companies.

Like Albany, much of the rail infrastructure was concentrated at one end of the city. The union railroad stations have always been located near the intersection of present-day Erie Boulevard and Liberty Street. A roundhouse and maintenance facilities for the New York Central were built near the Mohawk River bridge to Scotia. Other yards near Seneca Street and along Maple Avenue were also close to the Mohawk River.

Schenectady County was growing rapidly at the beginning of the 20th century, with a population of 125,000 in 1930 (compared to 12,000 a hundred years earlier). Much of the growth was due to the expansion of General Electric, which eventually employed tens of thousands of people. The early railroads were gradually consolidated into several interstate lines, including the Delaware & Hudson, the New York Central, the West Shore, and the Boston & Maine. Nearby communities such as Delanson and Rotterdam Junction became important rail centers with freight yards, interchange tracks, and locomotive facilities.

After the first Schenectady station burned down in 1843, a temporary structure was quickly thrown together. In contrast to the stately station that it replaced, the new one was a low, rambling building containing two waiting rooms (one for men and one for women) and a ticket office between them. No one seemed to be in a hurry to replace the "temporary" station, as it was still in use 40 years later. (Efner History Center archives.)

Austin Yates, editor of *Schenectady County: Its History to the Close of the Nineteenth Century*, described the second station as "an architecturally miserable, unsightly, inconvenient little horror." He went on to lament that it "retarded Schenectady's progress for many years. The wayfarer averted his gaze while the Schenectadian came to it in horror and fled from it in disgust." (Efner History Center archives.)

This 1875 view of Schenectady shows most of the important rail-related infrastructure in the city. The Schenectady Locomotive Works at left has not yet expanded to the west side of the Erie Canal. The New York Central's John Street roundhouse and yard is at center, leading to the Mohawk River bridge to Scotia. The narrow, rambling union station is at the top right among the railroad tracks. (Library of Congress.)

Public complaints and newspaper editorials finally had their effect, and a new station was built by the New York Central in 1885. The decorative brick building, with its ornate roof design, was a vast improvement over its predecessor. However, the station was doomed when it was decided in 1900 to raise many railroad tracks above street level throughout the city. (Efner History Center archives.)

The Niskayuna station was built in 1843 on the Troy & Schenectady Railroad. It was a busy place for its size, processing about 100 passengers a day for many years. It was rebuilt to its present form in 1880 and survives to the present day. Nearby was a water tower for steam engines and sidings for dropping off freight cars. Quarry stone and products from local farmers were loaded here. (Chris Morley collection.)

The *Empire State Express* was the New York Central's answer to passengers' demands for a fast trip from New York City to Buffalo with limited stops. One of those trains is shown here outside Schenectady pulled by the famous land speed record-breaking locomotive No. 999. (Albany Public Library.)

The arrival of Thomas Edison's General Electric (GE) Company in 1886 transformed Schenectady, creating tens of thousands of new jobs by the early 1900s. A view of GE overlooking Broadway in 1912 shows its immense scale. It was by far the single largest business on the Delaware & Hudson. There was a total of nearly 20 miles of standard-gauge and narrow-gauge track running throughout the complex. (New York State Archives.)

After a fatal New York City train accident in 1902, the legislature banned steam locomotives within city limits. In response, ALCO was tasked by the New York Central to build a new type of electric locomotive, with General Electric supplying the equipment. The result was locomotive No. 6000. Between 1904 and 1906, this engine accumulated 50,000 miles on the test track near the GE plant. (New York State Library.)

The "railroad highway" between Schenectady and Saratoga Springs saw heavy traffic, especially during the summer tourist season. A Delaware & Hudson fast mail and express train headed by locomotive No. 445 is seen speeding north toward Saratoga around 1905. (Joseph A. Smith collection.)

The Delaware & Hudson and New York Central Troy branch main lines along Maxon Road were raised a few years after this photograph was taken, separating the tracks and road by a steep embankment. The siding has since been removed, but one track still exists today. (New York State Archives.)

A view of Union Street in Schenectady shows the multitude of railroad tracks before they were raised above street level. The bridge girders to the right and ahead are going over the Erie Canal. The large brick building was the Union School, no longer standing, while a crossing guard shanty can be seen behind a tree. (New York State Archives.)

There were numerous complaints and accidents concerning the many railroad crossings in Schenectady, which was growing rapidly in the late 1800s due to the expansion of General Electric. In 1900, it was decided to raise the tracks along Maxon Road and the Erie Canal above street level. Busy streets such as State (pictured), Union, Nott, and Liberty were soon much safer. (Efner History Center archives.)

Men are shown here in 1905 working near State and Dock Streets for the track-raising project. Dock Street once ran parallel to the Erie Canal but no longer exists. The building on the right, blocked by a Schenectady Railway trolley car, is the Barhyte & Devenpeck coal company. (New York State Archives.)

The $1.3-million track-raising project is under way in this 1903 scene. This view is from the Erie Canal looking east toward Broadway. The low building just beyond the tracks with the railcars in front of it is the coal, wood, and flour firm of Charles Rankin. The houses on top of the hill in the distance are on Summit Avenue. (Efner History Center archives.)

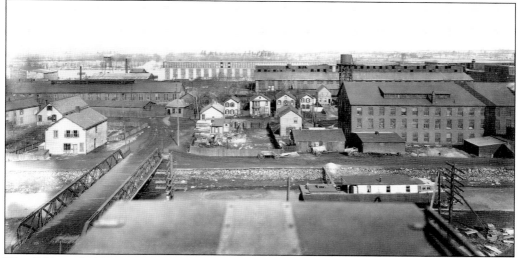

The 1880s and 1890s were a period of continued growth as the Schenectady Locomotive Works managed to survive a turbulent time in the locomotive industry. Smaller builders were closing all over the country, unable to compete against the likes of Baldwin Locomotive Works of Philadelphia. Schenectady managed to recruit talented designers and carry out facility upgrades to remain competitive. (Efner History Center archives.)

This 1917 view is looking east up Nott Street from the Erie Canal. The turntable was owned by ALCO and located on the northern corner of Maxon Road and Nott Street. Employees are seen marching for a Liberty bond parade. Storage tracks for new locomotives led off the turntable out of view on the left. This area would later become a diesel shop and much later (2010) the headquarters of the Golub Corporation. (Efner History Center archives.)

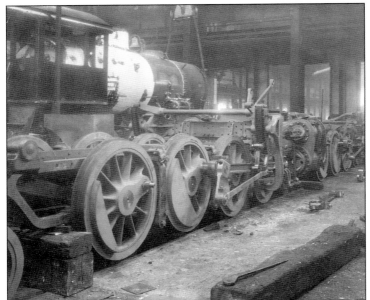

The growth of the Schenectady plant continued after its merger with the American Locomotive Company. In 1907, it set a production record by building 942 locomotives with a workforce of 6,200. These engines had an average retail price of approximately $20,000 each. The technical development of the steam locomotive now rapidly moved toward its all-time peak in the refinement of the Mallet articulated locomotives. (Rachel Clothier collection.)

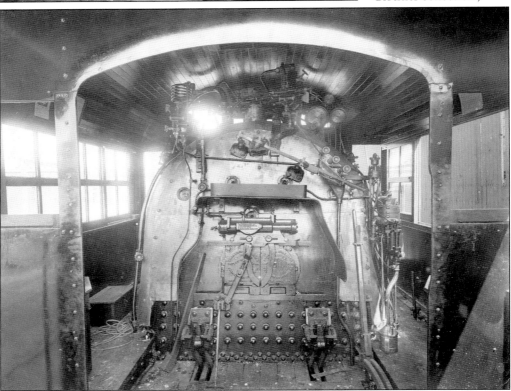

Only ALCO employees would normally see this view of a locomotive firebox in the midst of fabrication. Despite the huge size of steam locomotives in the early to mid-1900s, most of the interior room was occupied by the boiler, firebox, and controls, leaving little room for the engineer and fireman. Forward visibility was lacking as well. (Rachel Clothier collection.)

An example of the popular ALCO Niagara is New York Central locomotive No. 6008. It was built in 1945 to be used for hauling such famous passenger trains as the *Empire State Express* and *Twentieth Century Limited* at 100 miles an hour. Although these locomotives were dependable and efficient, they were retired and scrapped only 10 years later as diesels came into wide use. (Efner History Center archives.)

Some ALCO buildings and the double track main line can be seen in this view looking north along Maxon Road, near the intersection of Peek Street. The large gas holder tank, constructed in 1930, is on Seneca Street. Gas fuel was manufactured in Troy and piped to Schenectady for local use. It was removed in 1961. (Efner History Center archives.)

The historic part of Schenectady, near the Mohawk River, has been subjected to flooding for centuries. The so-called Easter Flood in March 1913 was one of the worst, caused by massive amounts of rain falling on frozen ground and swelling the river to historic levels. Since the ALCO plant was situated on the banks of the river, it suffered great damage and inconvenience. (Efner History Center archives.)

The massive extent of the American Locomotive Company plant is shown in this aerial photograph. It occupies land along both sides of the former Erie Canal (at this point Erie Boulevard). A railroad track can be seen snaking its way along the bank of the Mohawk River at the back of the property. ALCO's all-time annual production peak of steam locomotives occurred in 1944, when 1,354 were built. (Efner History Center archives.)

The largest locomotive ever built was the 4-8-8-4 "Big Boy," manufactured by ALCO Schenectady. The Union Pacific (UP) needed the most powerful engine possible to haul long trains over the Wasatch Range between Utah and Wyoming. The first of 25 Class 4000 Big Boys was delivered to the UP in September 1940. Each cost $265,000, equivalent to over $4.5 million today. (Chris Morley collection.)

A Big Boy locomotive is shown in the process of manufacture inside the ALCO Schenectady shop. It was so big that the Union Pacific Railroad had to realign curves, install heavier track, and lengthen turntables in many places. The design was based on the successful Challenger series of 4-6-6-4 articulated locomotives, also built by ALCO. (Chris Morley collection.)

In 1936, the New York Central sent a "normal" ALCO-built Mohawk 4-8-2 locomotive to the West Albany Shops to receive custom cladding for the Rexall Train national tour, a traveling exhibition for the United Drug Company. It took 30 days of double work shifts to complete the labor-intensive conversion. Later that year, more than two million people turned out to see the streamlined, blue and white locomotive and its 12 heavyweight Pullman cars. (Chris Morley collection.)

The Ringling Bros. and Barnum & Bailey circus train (shown here unloading in Schenectady) was always a welcome sight. A typical train in the 1890s consisted of 4 custom-designed animal stock cars, 33 passenger cars for the performers, 2 container cars, and 17 flatcars for equipment. The circus train came to Schenectady for the last time in 1956. (New York State Archives.)

The Boston & Maine, the New York Central, and the West Shore Railroads all connected at Rotterdam Junction, where yards were established to interchange freight. Until the construction of the Carman Cutoff and Selkirk Yard in the 1920s, Rotterdam Junction was the only place where the New York Central connected with its West Shore subsidiary. (Joseph A. Smith collection.)

The Boston & Maine Railroad constructed a sprawling 30-track rail yard extending from near the historic Mabee Farm to present-day Route 5S. During its heyday, Rotterdam Junction boasted a roundhouse, passenger station, tavern, slaughterhouse, schoolhouse, several hotels, and even its own short-lived newspaper. In 1931, the yard and 550 workers were relocated to Mechanicville in Saratoga County, ending the hamlet's glory days of railroading. (Chris Morley collection.)

The name Delanson comes from a contraction of Delaware & Hudson. A combined passenger station and a freight depot were built after tracks were laid by the Albany & Susquehanna Railroad in the 1860s. The station burned down in 1882, but a handsome new one was built in its place (shown). Delaware & Hudson gas-electric engine No. 2000, made by General Electric, is parked out front. (John Nehrich; Dean Splittgerber collection.)

The Delaware & Hudson established Delanson as a locomotive repair and refueling point, building a roundhouse for this purpose. By the early 1900s, the hamlet had a lumberyard, blacksmith, creamery, sawmill, two hotels, and large freight yards. Locomotive servicing was discontinued in the 1930s. (Chris Morley collection.)

In Schenectady, the New York Central main line (at top right) crossed over Broadway (then known as Center Street). The large structure on the left still exists (constructed as the Micanite Works in 1915), while all the buildings adjacent have been torn down due to landslides on the hill behind. Note the coal-unloading platforms at the top right and right side of the photograph. (Efner History Center archives.)

When the Delaware & Hudson built this brick freight house in 1880, it was level with both the Erie Canal on one side and the train tracks on the other. New spur tracks had to be constructed from the elevated main line to the rear of the building in 1905. This view is the backside of the building, with the main line behind the photographer. (Chris Morley collection.)

The roundhouse and small yard near John Street in Schenectady was built by the New York Central soon after it combined with other railroads in 1853. It was used for light locomotive repairs and maintenance but had been abandoned by the time this picture was taken and was torn down soon after. (Efner History Center archives.)

The Mohawk River Bridge, shown here in the 1940s, is still in use by the railroads. This view is looking north on the Delaware & Hudson main line heading to Mohawk Yard in East Glenville. From there the tracks continue north to Saratoga Springs or northeast to the Mechanicville classification yard. (Efner History Center archives.)

When the main line was raised above street level, the 15-year-old brick passenger station had to be torn down. However, in 1908, a grand Neoclassical-style union station was constructed in its place by the New York Central & Hudson River Railroad. This view from Wall Street shows the station next to the Edison Hotel, which faced State Street. (Efner History Center archives.)

The new Schenectady Union Station was built at a cost of $2 million over a period of three years. A large parking lot was located on the Wall Street side to accommodate large numbers of carriages. Attached to the station were the railway express warehouse and an elegant arcade (right). The tracks ran on top of the wall at left. (Efner History Center archives.)

The massive interior of the Schenectady Union Station measured 23,000 square feet. The gleaming marble walls were supported by stone columns that projected opulence and grandeur. Amenities such as lounges, a snack counter, a newsstand, and restrooms provided every modern convenience. The men's and women's lounges were finished with hardwood and paneled ceilings, cement plastered walls, and terrazzo flooring with marble strips. Large clocks at either end of the waiting room gave the time from both inside and out. (Both, Efner History Center archives.)

This trackside view of the Schenectady Union Station shows the Edison Hotel in the distance and the passenger waiting platforms in the foreground. The multitude of tracks belong to the Delaware & Hudson and the New York Central Railroads. (Efner History Center archives.)

Pres. Harry Truman visited the Schenectady Union Station on October 10, 1952. He gave a short, 10-minute speech in support of Democratic presidential hopeful Adlai Stevenson in front of a large crowd of 2,500. Other presidents who visited Schenectady via the New York Central over the years included Abraham Lincoln, William McKinley, Teddy Roosevelt, Franklin Roosevelt, and Dwight D. Eisenhower. (Chris Morley collection.)

Saratoga Springs was already a famous vacation resort before the Saratoga & Schenectady Railroad arrived in 1833. Because travel to Saratoga and nearby Ballston Spa was so slow and difficult, most vacationers arrived in early June and remained until September, to the delight of area hotel owners. This tradition ended after the railroad went into service, but the number of summer visitors doubled in 1834 and continued to increase. This 1931 scene of the Saratoga station (left) looking over Church Street shows Railroad Avenue in front of the station and a glimpse of the six-track yard behind. (Saratoga Springs Public Library.)

# Four

# TROY AND VICINITY

The city of Troy enjoyed a large commerce in iron, steel, stoves, collars, and cuffs from the mid-1800s to the mid-1900s. In addition to the railroads and canals that brought materials into and out of the city, there were two steamboat lines and one canal barge line that plied the Hudson River. The New York Central connected in Troy with the Boston & Maine to the east, the Rutland Railroad to Vermont, and the Delaware & Hudson to Saratoga, Plattsburg, and Montreal to the north. The city was also a major terminating point for tourists heading to the North Country. Resort areas such as Ausable Chasm, Blue Mountain Lake, Chester, Hadley, Keene Valley, and Lake Placid were all reached by disembarking a New York Central train at Troy and then catching a Delaware & Hudson train to Saratoga, Port Kent, or other stations.

The Troy Union Railroad, which was a partnership of the major railroads that operated within the city, was formed in 1851 to build a union station on Sixth Avenue and divert the main line from River Street to the new station. The Rensselaer & Saratoga, the Schenectady & Troy, the Troy & Boston, and the Troy & Greenbush each contributed toward the cost. The tracks on River Street were torn up, while new tracks were constructed to the Green Island Bridge, allowing steam engines to pass over it for the first time.

Unlike other cities that rerouted tracks or elevated them over city streets, the people of Troy lived with a main line that came within a few feet of dozens of buildings. Despite the Trojans' love of their railroads, the union station was plagued by bad luck. The roof partially collapsed in 1859, the entire station burned down in 1862, and in 1898, it had to be demolished due to structural decay. The stately Georgian version that replaced the train shed–style station was more fortunate, lasting until passenger operations ceased. After the last union station was demolished in 1959, it was not long before all of the tracks were removed from Troy streets, leaving only a few odd-shaped buildings behind as evidence that railroads ever operated within the city.

The city of Troy has experienced devastating fires in its history. The fire of 1862 started on the wooden Rensselaer & Saratoga Railroad (Green Island) bridge and spread eastward, destroying hundreds of structures, including the recently rebuilt union station. This view is looking west toward the Hudson River. (Library of Congress.)

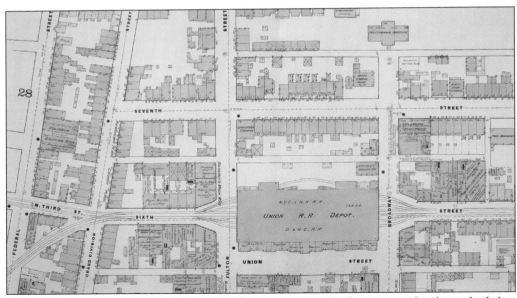

The third union station was rebuilt much the same way as the first two, with a large shed that completely sheltered passenger trains. The front side of the structure, facing Union Street, contained the waiting room, baggage rooms, restrooms, and company offices. This 1885 map shows the layout of the station as well as the close quarters of surrounding buildings even at this early date. (Sanborn maps, Library of Congress.)

The train shed was an impressive sight to passengers, but fumes from the steam locomotives must have been intense. This view of the third union station looking down Broadway (right) shows the five arched door openings that each admitted two trains. To the left is the front of the building facing Union Street. The original station had four-story towers on either end rather than two. (Hart Cluett Museum of Historic Rensselaer County collection.)

The roof of the train shed covering the side tracks had to be torn down in 1898 because gas from the steam engines had eaten away at the supporting trusses. Rather than replacing the roof, the Troy Union Railroad decided a more modern station was needed. The large train shed–style depot had fallen out of favor by that time. (Joseph A. Smith collection.)

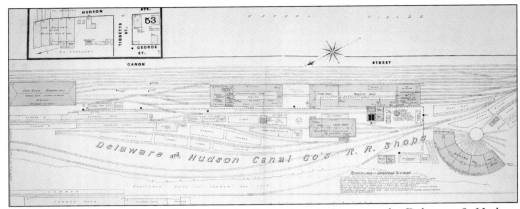

Once the site of a small roundhouse for the Rensselaer & Saratoga, the Delaware & Hudson built significant fabrication and repair shops here on Tibbits Avenue in Green Island in 1871. This 1885 building layout shows the car repair shop, construction shop, and machine shop. The roundhouse was upgraded from the original 8-stall structure to the 15-stall facility shown. Two hundred men were employed here at this time. (Sanborn maps, Library of Congress.)

In 1890, the three shops noted above were combined into one 750-foot-long structure. The locomotive facility on the far right had five bays, while behind were the machine, forge, and car fabrication shops. The second floor was used for wood work and storage. Just to the west was a 52,000-gallon water tank enclosed by brick walls. The buildings were abandoned by the time this picture was taken. (Library of Congress.)

On the east side of the railroad bridge in Green Island was an impressive array of railroad infrastructure. The Delaware & Hudson, the New York Central, and the United Traction Company all had passenger and freight stations at the same intersection. The Delaware & Hudson station, shown here, was built in 1890 and torn down in 1938. (John Nehrich; Hart Cluett Museum of Historic Rensselaer County collection.)

The Troy & Schenectady Railroad (later New York Central) built this Greek Revival–inspired station in Green Island. Note the Doric (squared) columns in the corners and doorways. It was rare to see this style of station still standing in the 1930s. Next door on the right, mostly out of the picture, was the freight house. (Gino DiCarlo; Jeff English/Joe Carlin collection.)

The firm of Eaton and Gilbert built the first eight-wheeled passenger cars for the Troy & Schenectady Railroad, among many others. After the plant was destroyed by fire in 1854, the property was sold to the Troy Union Railroad for the new station. Uri Gilbert then moved operations to Green Island, where more space was available. By the late 1800s, as many as 80 passenger cars were in various stages of production at a time. (Author's collection.)

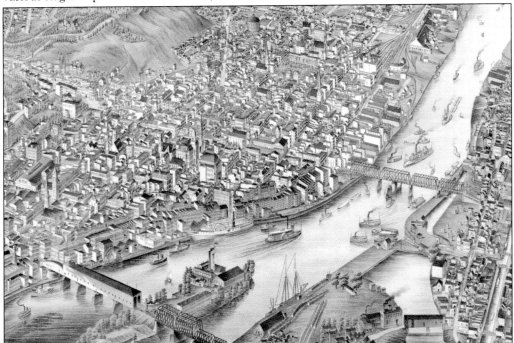

This 1881 overview of Troy shows the railroad bridge (bottom) from Green Island to Troy. The original bridge burned in 1862, taking part of downtown Troy with it. At left is the rounded train shed of the union station. A small yard and roundhouse is located near Adams Street on the east bank of the Hudson River. (Library of Congress.)

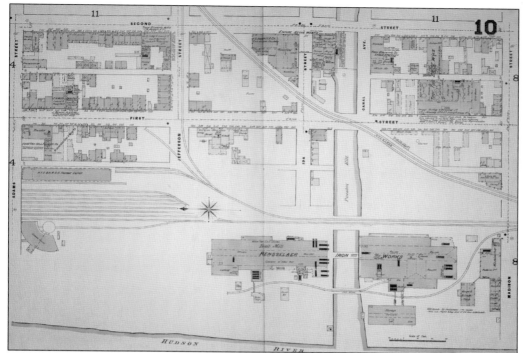

This 1885 insurance map shows the Adams Street engine house and freight depot of the New York Central. A few years later, more storage tracks were added in the space below the yard. The Rensselaer Iron Works was nearby with its own spur track. The mill turned out thousands of miles of iron rail as well as parts for the Union navy's ironclad Civil War ship *Monitor*. (Sanborn maps, Library of Congress.)

The railroad YMCA building offered a gymnasium and free books to read for train crews laying over at Troy. The sloping train shed roof of the union station is at left. This photograph was taken about 10 years after the YMCA was built in 1882. (Joseph A. Smith collection.)

The final Troy Union Station was built in 1903 after the former train shed station had to be demolished. The beautiful Beaux-Arts and Georgian-style structure was on par with the grand stations of Albany and Schenectady. This view of Union Street shows the stately facade, with trolley tracks just visible on the bottom left. (Library of Congress.)

The Troy Union Station was a gathering place on many occasions, such as soldiers leaving or returning from war. The mass of soldiers here is departing for France in 1918 to experience the horrors of trench warfare. Luckily the war ended soon after they arrived in Europe. (Hart Cluett Museum of Historic Rensselaer County collection.)

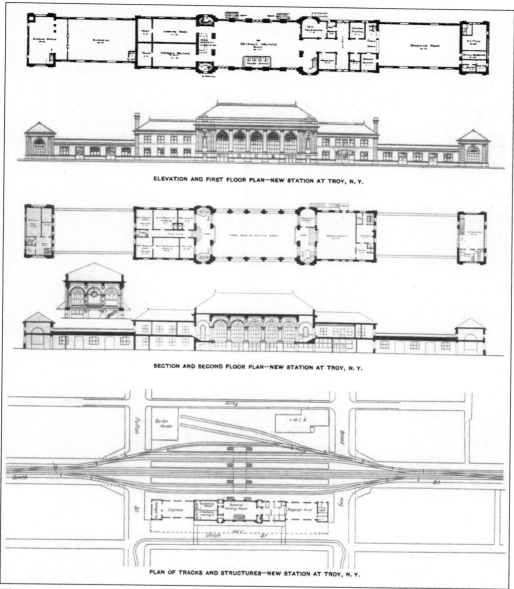

ELEVATION AND FIRST FLOOR PLAN—NEW STATION AT TROY, N. Y.

SECTION AND SECOND FLOOR PLAN—NEW STATION AT TROY, N. Y.

PLAN OF TRACKS AND STRUCTURES—NEW STATION AT TROY, N. Y.

This elevation plan of the union station shows the large central waiting room and ticket office flanked by men's and women's lounges, an express room at left, and a baggage room at right. The bottom diagram shows the track layout along Sixth Avenue and four waiting platforms for the 130 different passenger trains that came through each day. The boiler house and railroad YMCA were situated on the east side of the tracks. (Author's collection.)

The interior of the Troy Union Station matched the grandeur of the union stations in Schenectady and Albany. The steps on the right lead to the subway that went under the tracks to the passenger trains. The entrance and ticket windows are at left. (Both, Joseph A. Smith collection.)

These views of the Troy Union Station are below ground. The stairs led from the waiting room main lobby to the pedestrian subway and passenger train tracks. There were eight parallel tracks next to the station on Sixth Avenue at that time. (Both, Joseph A. Smith collection.)

These two views show the track side of the Troy Union Station looking over Sixth Avenue. The "umbrella roofed" platforms were much different than the giant train shed that sheltered passengers since 1853. These tracks saw dozens of trains a day, especially those of the Belt Line that ran between Troy and Albany at half-hour intervals. (Both, Joseph A. Smith collection.)

This unusual view of the Troy Union Station (extreme left), taken on Broadway facing east, overlooks the main line tracks. The railroad YMCA reading room building is on the left. Straight ahead in the distance is Seventh Avenue and the Rensselaer Polytechnic Institute on top of the hill. (Joseph A. Smith collection.)

Ahead is the railroad tunnel under the Congress and Ferry Street Block along Sixth Avenue. The tunnel was later bricked up but survived intact until 2009, when it was filled in for an economic development project. At left is a railroad shanty, required for each and every crossing in the city. (Joseph A. Smith collection.)

An interlocking tower locked a series of signals and levers so that a train on a specific track would automatically be navigated through dozens of switches. Four of these towers were needed in Troy. Towers 1 and 2 controlled the approaches to the station. Tower 3 (shown) was located on Fifth Avenue and controlled the west-side wye tracks, while Tower 4 controlled the north-side tracks. (Joseph A. Smith collection.)

A train is seen pulling into the Troy Union Station from the Broadway side. Space was so tight on Sixth Avenue that the interlocking towers (one of them seen at far right) had to be built over the tracks. On the corner is the garage of Fred Lowe, who was also a Troy funeral director for 40 years. (Hart Cluett Museum of Historic Rensselaer County collection.)

In 1827, Hannah Montague invented the detachable collar at her home on Third Street and spawned an entire industry. By the late 1800s, detachable collars were used around the country, and the industry employed some 15,000 people in Troy alone. The Emigh & Straub collar factory at 405 Federal Street was one of about two dozen. Tower 3 on Fifth Avenue is seen on the right. (Hart Cluett Museum of Historic Rensselaer County collection.)

Adams Street Station, south of the union station, was a waiting room that serviced South Troy and its thousands of factory workers. Here, the Troy & Greenbush Railroad built a freight house, machine shop, turntable, and yards along both sides of River Street. These facilities were destroyed by fire in 1854. (Chris Morley collection.)

This view of Sixth Avenue is facing south from Jacob Street, showing the tracks of the Boston & Maine (formerly Troy & Boston). Just ahead would be the switch that either led right toward the Green Island Bridge or straight to the Troy Union Station. (Hart Cluett Museum of Historic Rensselaer County collection.)

Here is another view looking down Sixth Avenue, this time from Federal Street in 1912. This stretch of track lay between the Green Island Bridge over the Hudson River and the Troy Union Station. The original Rensselaer & Saratoga Railroad of 1835 terminated near here on River Street. Not many cities tolerated dozens of trains rumbling down main thoroughfares by this time. (Joseph A. Smith collection.)

Delaware & Hudson locomotive No. 652, manufactured at the Colonie Shops in 1929, is seen pulling into the Troy Union Station over Fulton Street. On the right is the Tolhurst Machine Works, which was part of the General Laundry Machine Corporation. The building was torn down in 1950, about 10 years after this picture was taken. (Hart Cluett Museum of Historic Rensselaer County collection.)

The Troy & Boston; the Boston, Hoosac Tunnel & Western; and the Greenwich & Johnsonville Railroads connected here in Johnsonville, strategically located on the Hoosick River between Eagle Bridge and Schaghticoke. The Johnsonville Axe Manufacturing Company was one of the largest axe makers in the region, producing hundreds of thousands a year for the railroads to deliver. (Author's collection.)

In Rensselaer County, the Boston & Maine Railroad maintained a multitude of stations. Some of them included Eagle Bridge, Buskirk, Hoosick Falls, Johnsonville, Schaghticoke, and the small hamlet of Melrose, shown here. A number of homes were built in Melrose as summer retreats for wealthy Troy businessmen. This station somehow survived being demolished and is now a residence. (Chris Kelly, Schaghticoke town historian collection.)

The Boston & Maine operated into Hoosick Falls, 27 miles northeast of Troy, while a small trolley line to Bennington and Pittsfield was provided by the Bennington & North Adams Street Railway, chartered in 1903. The principal manufactures were knit goods, shirts, and agricultural machinery. The railroad station also handled crops grown in the surrounding countryside, especially potatoes. (Joseph A. Smith collection.)

The first primitive Troy & Boston station at Lansingburgh was followed by a more proper one in 1858 on the east end of 115th Street. Pictured is the version built by the Boston & Maine in 1908. After passenger service was discontinued, the building was used by a coal dealer until being torn down in 1974. (Joseph A. Smith collection.)

The Boston & Maine Railroad was double-tracking the line between Troy and Johnsonville in the spring of 1907 when locomotive No. 1045 somehow derailed and fell down the embankment. Today, this is Oil Mill Hill Road. (Joseph A. Smith collection.)

The little town of Petersburgh in eastern Rensselaer County hosted several early railroads, including the Lebanon Springs; the Troy & Bennington; the Troy & Boston; and the Boston, Hoosac Tunnel & Western. Petersburgh Junction (pictured) hosted the Boston & Maine and was part of the Rutland Railroad's famous Corkscrew Division, known for its many turns and grades. (Joseph A. Smith collection.)

In addition to the large classification yard at Mechanicville, the former Boston & Troy freight yard was maintained by the Boston & Maine near Middleburgh Street in Troy. A roundhouse, several freight depots, and dozens of tracks formed a complex that served as the railroad's eastern freight terminal. Shown is a derailment in July 1912. (Joseph A. Smith collection.)

The large cotton and knitting exports of Cohoes warranted separate passenger and freight houses, both of which were built in 1852 on Oneida Street with the arrival of the Albany Northern Railroad. A new passenger station was built in 1883 on Van Rensselaer Street, while the freight house lasted until 1912, when it was replaced with a larger structure. Both buildings still stand today. (Chris Morley collection.)

Members of a railroad section crew, sometimes called "gandy dancers," pose in their work cars just north of the Cohoes station in 1947. The photographer was standing on Pine Street facing west, looking over the Van Rensselaer Street intersection. The Presbyterian church at right and the square building next to it (then a YWCA) still stand. (John Nehrich; Delaware & Hudson collection.)

There were many large mills and factories along the Hudson River in Troy. When the iron foundries changed from waterpower to coal for fuel, new coal processing plants were needed. The pictured Niagara-Mohawk furnace manufactured coke fuel that was used in nearby factories such as the Burden Iron Works. This c. 1940 view is looking north from the Menands Bridge. (Hart Cluett Museum of Historic Rensselaer County collection.)

The Rutland Railroad had track rights over the Boston & Maine, the Troy Union, and the New York Central Railroads in New York State. Locomotive No. 90, photographed at the Boston & Maine roundhouse on Eighth Street in Troy, was built by ALCO Schenectady in 1946. (Hart Cluett Museum of Historic Rensselaer County collection.)

# Five

# CHANGING TIMES

The Capital District's railroad industry reached its peak in the beginning of the 1900s. Tens of thousands of people found steady work with the railroads themselves and related industries such as manufacturing locomotives, cars, and track rails.

The first blow to Capital District rail operations was the New York Central's Castleton Cut-Off project. Due to the steep hill at West Albany that often required extra locomotives, a new bridge was built over the Hudson River in Castleton, south of Albany, as well as a double-track rail line that traveled northwest to Schenectady, completely bypassing the Albany area. In addition, a new classification yard was built along this corridor at Selkirk. Thereafter, the yards of Rensselaer, the Albany waterfront, and West Albany all declined in importance.

As trucking superseded hauling freight by rail and personal automobiles all but killed off the passenger trains in the years following World War II, employment in rail facilities steadily declined. The repair and fabrication shops at Green Island, West Albany, and Colonie are now becoming distant memories after closing down decades ago.

Both the Delaware & Hudson and the Boston & Maine systems went into receivership during the 1960s as passenger traffic dropped and trucking companies began to haul more freight cross-country. In 1968, the unthinkable occurred when the New York Central was merged with its historic rival, the Pennsylvania Railroad, to form Penn Central and suddenly disappeared into history.

Although Capital District railroading experienced a painful period of decline, the public has come to accept rail lines as an efficient way to transport people and freight. The Albany-Rensselaer Station is one of Amtrak's top 10 busiest stations. The Pan Am Railways yard at Mechanicville was expanded in 2012 on the site of the former Boston & Maine yard. In 2018, a new passenger station was built in Schenectady that is reminiscent of the one that was lost nearly half a century ago. The classification yard at Selkirk remains an important facility in the CSX Transportation system. The Port of Albany also continues to provide freight business to CSX and the Canadian Pacific Railway.

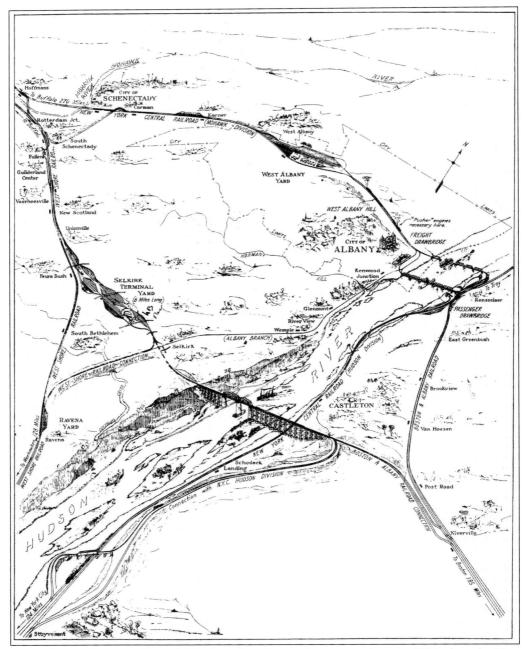

A significant change in Capital District railroad operations came about in 1924 when the New York Central finished the Castleton Cut-Off project. This map shows how the new bridge over the Hudson River and a yard at Selkirk resulted in most traffic bypassing the Capital District altogether. Freight trains also no longer had to wait for boats to float by before the bridges at Maiden Lane and Livingston Avenue could open to the railroads. (New York State Archives.)

The Alfred H. Smith Memorial Bridge at Castleton was meant to be a "high bridge" with a river clearance of 135 feet. Boats of all sizes could then pass under it without interrupting rail operations. This photograph was taken a few years after it was built. Even today, all trains from New York City heading to points west must use this bridge. (New York State Archives.)

When operations began at the Selkirk Yard in 1924, various industry publications described it as "one of the greatest and most up-to-date gravity freight classification yards in existence." It was constructed on a flat area six miles long and one mile wide to accommodate the longest trains. The 250 miles of track could theoretically hold 20,000 cars, although the yard was designed to process 8,000 per day. (New York State Library.)

In addition to its great size, the Selkirk Yard contained two roundhouses that were each capable of holding 30 of the largest locomotives. The engine terminal also had two 600-ton coal bins fed by conveyors and seven ash pits. A machine shop, storehouse, mechanical shop, and powerhouse were all built adjacent to the roundhouses. (Joseph Boehlke, Ravena-Coeymans Historical Society collection.)

The SK interlocking tower at Selkirk can be seen in the upper right side of this 1930s photograph. The tower was located at the east end of the yard near the present-day Route 9W overpass. Until centralized traffic control was implemented, an operator in the tower manually set the appropriate signals (stop, caution, proceed, etc.) at this busy main line junction. (Chris Morley collection.)

In 1925, the Port of Albany was created to replace the aging Albany Basin. It was the nearest all-year Atlantic seaport to the Great Lakes and a natural point for transshipment of foreign and domestic commerce originating in New York State and northern New England. The pictured Cargill grain elevator could hold 13 million bushels and handled 12 railroad cars a day. (John Nehrich; Delaware & Hudson collection.)

Direct interchange facilities between ships and railroads were constructed at the Port of Albany that remain today. A British cargo ship is docked at the port in 1940, not long before the United States entered World War II. The railroads handled such bulk items as animal feed, wood pulp, steel, molasses, and grain. (New York State Archives.)

The last steam locomotive to be repaired at the West Albany Shops was the Hudson class No. 5270 on September 25, 1952. Activity in West Albany gradually declined in favor of the newly equipped shops at Selkirk, Harmon, and Collinwood, Ohio. At that time, there were only about 200 employees, down from 1,500 a few years earlier. (Chris Morley collection.)

Commodore Vanderbilt preferred to use Wagner sleeping cars on the New York Central, but in 1900, the Wagner Palace Car Company was sold to the Pullman Car Company. Pullman passenger cars can still be seen in this 1950 photograph of the Albany Union Station. Later in the decade, they would be replaced by standard coaches to reduce costs. (Joseph A. Smith collection.)

The upper-level tracks shown at the Albany station were used by the New York Central, while the lower tracks were used by the Delaware & Hudson and the West Shore Railroads. The Central Warehouse building is on the far right. Diesel locomotives have plainly taken over switching and passenger service duties at the time of this late-1950s photograph. (Albany Public Library.)

An aerial view of the Albany waterfront shows a mass of automobiles and buses, a sure sign that the public was enjoying the freedom of owning a personal vehicle rather than relying on train schedules. The Delaware & Hudson office building is at the bottom center of the photograph, while the union station is left of center. (Chris Morley collection.)

117

Some passenger cars were starting to look their age by the time this picture was taken at the Albany Union Station in 1968. Ahead is the Central Warehouse, built in 1922 to store meats and dry goods in an era before refrigeration. A spur track near the Livingston Avenue Bridge ran right into the structure. It was made with so much steel and concrete that it stands today as a landmark and eyesore. (New York State Library.)

The outlines of two roundhouses and the Flour House can be seen in this 1962 aerial photograph looking west from Rensselaer. On the left side of Maiden Lane Bridge was the New York Central roundhouse, while on the extreme right side was the Boston & Albany roundhouse. The yards are a shadow of what they once were before most operations were diverted to the Selkirk Yard. (Albany Public Library.)

118

Once the New York Central and the West Shore switched to diesel power, the need for roundhouses disappeared. One of the roundhouses in Selkirk is abandoned in this 1960 photograph. Only one small roundhouse survives today (in Troy) of the many that once dotted the landscape. (New York State Library.)

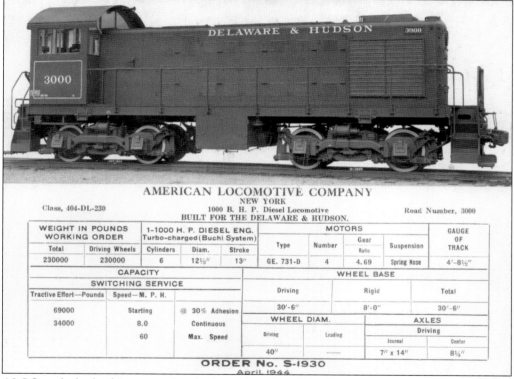

## AMERICAN LOCOMOTIVE COMPANY
### NEW YORK
1000 B. H. P. Diesel Locomotive
#### BUILT FOR THE DELAWARE & HUDSON.

Class, 404-DL-230     Road Number, 3000

| WEIGHT IN POUNDS WORKING ORDER | | 1-1000 H. P. DIESEL ENG. Turbo-charged (Buchi System) | | | MOTORS | | | | GAUGE OF TRACK |
|---|---|---|---|---|---|---|---|---|---|
| Total | Driving Wheels | Cylinders | Diam. | Stroke | Type | Number | Gear Ratio | Suspension | |
| 230000 | 230000 | 6 | 12½″ | 13″ | GE. 731-D | 4 | 4.69 | Spring Nose | 4′-8½″ |

| CAPACITY | | | | | WHEEL BASE | | |
|---|---|---|---|---|---|---|---|
| SWITCHING SERVICE | | | | | Driving | Rigid | Total |
| Tractive Effort—Pounds | Speed—M. P. H. | | | | 30′-6″ | 8′-0″ | 30′-6″ |
| 69000 | Starting | @ 30% Adhesion | | | WHEEL DIAM. | | AXLES |
| 34000 | 8.0 | Continuous | | | Driving | Leading | Driving |
| | 60 | Max. Speed | | | | | Journal | Center |
| | | | | | 40″ | — | 7″ x 14″ | 8¼″ |

#### ORDER No. S-1930
April, 1944

ALCO took the lead in new technologies and produced the first commercially successful diesel engine in 1924. It benefited from partnering with its neighbor General Electric for supplying all of the electrical equipment, such as for this Delaware & Hudson 1,000-horsepower S-2 series. Despite some early successes, GE severed its relationship in 1953 and became a competitor, which ultimately played a role in ALCO's decline. (Chris Morley collection.)

The construction of highways was a harbinger of rough times ahead for the railroads. Here in the town of Colonie near Dunsbach Ferry, the Adirondack Northway (I-87) was constructed in 1960. The intersection of the New York Central's Troy branch was one of the few railroad highway crossings in the country. This line was abandoned a few years later. (Gino DiCarlo; Francis Poulin photograph, Jeff English collection.)

Pictured is the Grand Street and Sixth Avenue crossing in 1955. Automatic gates like the one shown at bottom left eliminated the need for crossing shanties and tenders. In much of Troy, the only vestiges of the railroads left today are angled buildings like these, which probably baffle those who do not know the history behind them. (John Nehrich; Jim Shaughnessy collection.)

This view of Troy Union Station overlooks Broadway. The Boston & Maine operated a dozen trains daily through the 1950s, including the *Minute Man, Green Mountain Flyer,* and *Mount Royal.* The Delaware & Hudson's New York–to–Montreal express train was the *Laurentian* during the day and the *Montreal Limited* at night. (Jim Shaughnessy collection.)

It was a sad day in Troy when the union station was demolished in 1959, ending all passenger service in that city for the first time in 125 years. Only a single track was left in place for the Rutland Railroad milk train to Chatham. Even this track was removed in 1964 after the Rutland was abandoned. (Joseph A. Smith collection.)

The Boston & Maine was the most active railroad in Troy during the mid-1900s. Pictured is Electro-Motive Division (EMD) SW1 diesel switcher No. 1114 in 1954. This engine was later used by the Guilford Rail System, a paper mill, Stone Mountain Scenic Railroad, and finally the Standridge Color Corporation in Georgia, where it still operates. (New York State Library, Fred Abele collection.)

The age of glamorous passenger trains was over, and soon the use of small stations such as this one in Hoosick Falls would be over as well. The Boston & Maine Railroad ended passenger service from Troy to Massachusetts in 1958, along with many other routes. All long distance passenger service ended two years later, although freight operations continued. (Joseph A. Smith collection.)

The once-opulent interior of the Schenectady Union Station was strewn with debris after it was officially closed in June 1969. A year earlier, the New York Central was absorbed by the Pennsylvania Railroad, which was desperate to cut costs wherever it could. Much to the dismay of Schenectady residents, a small station in Colonie was about to take the place of their beloved union station. (Efner History Center archives.)

There was some talk of saving the Schenectady Union Station, but the cost of rehabilitating such a large building for other uses proved to be prohibitive. It was torn down in February 1971 and turned into a parking lot. It would be eight years before a drab Amtrak station took its place and 50 years before a proper station was built. (Efner History Center archives.)

The Delaware & Hudson depot on Erie Boulevard survived longer than most freight stations. The original brick freight house and offices are at left and center, while hidden on the right is the 1900s addition. It served as a Grossman's Distribution Center from 1968 to 2009 but laid abandoned afterward and was finally torn down 10 years later. (Author's collection.)

There was some hope that diesel technology could save railroads from decline after World War II. The transformation of locomotive power from steam to diesel began on some railroads prior to the war, but because there was little money for capital improvements, the New York Central did not start the process until the late 1940s. A few are shown here at the aging Albany station in 1968. (New York State Library.)

Baggage wagons stand idle at Albany Union Station in 1968, a few months before it was closed by Penn Central. The Highway 787 construction project along the Hudson River was already under way, eradicating the Bull Run freight yard, coach yard, and Maiden Lane Bridge. (New York State Library.)

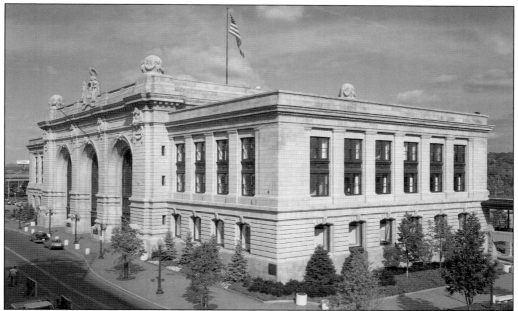

Unlike the union stations in Schenectady and Troy, the Albany station building was purchased by New York State in conjunction with the Highway 787 construction project and converted to other uses. It is listed in the National Register of Historic Places. The exterior looks much like it did when built 120 years ago. The former Delaware & Hudson office building also still stands. (Library of Congress.)

A new, much smaller station across the Hudson River at Rensselaer took the place of the Albany Union Station. A Penn Central train is seen idling shortly before the company declared bankruptcy in 1970. Since then, the Albany-Rensselaer Station has been rebuilt twice, in 1980 and 2002. (Chris Morley collection.)

The Delaware & Hudson logo on the locomotive was probably a comforting sight to remind people that this railroad was still operating, but sadly, the New York Central was history. It must have been disconcerting for the people of Albany to find their way across the Hudson River and wait at a station that was drab and utilitarian compared to the old union station. (Joseph A. Smith collection.)

Although the Green Island Shops were constructed during the early days of railroading, they continued to conduct light repairs well into the 1930s. For many years afterward, the surviving buildings sat vacant along the Delaware & Hudson line to Waterford. They were listed in the National Register of Historic Places but tragically caught fire in March 2011 and were demolished. This photograph was taken five months earlier. (Author's collection.)

ALCO lasted longer than most other locomotive builders but fell behind in sales to both EMD and General Electric. The Schenectady plant finally closed in 1969 after 120 years of operation. Some of the warehouses were used by GE until 2004. The site then lay vacant, turning into an eyesore along the Mohawk River. The buildings were finally torn down in 2014 for a mixed-use redevelopment project. (Author's collection.)

# DISCOVER THOUSANDS OF LOCAL HISTORY BOOKS
## FEATURING MILLIONS OF VINTAGE IMAGES

Arcadia Publishing, the leading local history publisher in the United States, is committed to making history accessible and meaningful through publishing books that celebrate and preserve the heritage of America's people and places.

## Find more books like this at
## www.arcadiapublishing.com

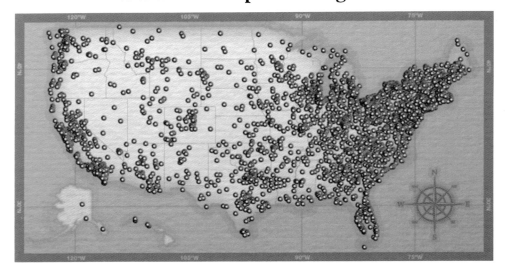

Search for your hometown history, your old stomping grounds, and even your favorite sports team.